LET'S
FACE IT

*Comments on LET'S FACE IT from outstanding
women in the fields of education, welfare,
public service, and entertainment.*

"Perhaps as many as eight out of ten girls who apply for jobs lack thorough knowledge in the area of good grooming....Therefore, Elsie Archer's book is a girl's best friend, and especially a friend to the girl who will follow the advice and practical guidance it offers."—DIAHANN CARROLL

"Elsie Archer presents the specifics of good grooming with an authority that reflects her wide experience. Even more important is the feeling of warmth and personal interest that reflects the awareness she has derived through helping girls develop greater self-confidence. The encouragement that girls will find between the covers of this book should be of both immediate and lasting value."—HAZEL OSBORN, *Institutional Consultant to the Federation of Protestant Welfare Agencies, Inc.*

"*Let's Face It* is a good-grooming guide and handbook that any young American girl can read to her advantage. Many adolescents, beset with the problems of 'growing up' will find understanding and sympathy in *Let's Face It*, and concrete things to do to help achieve their own personal identity.... Teen-agers will make this their handbook as they prepare for jobs and careers."—ANN TANNEYHILL, *Director of Vocational Services for the National Urban League*

"Girls should welcome this advice and counsel which comes in language that is neither patronizing not dictatorial....Girls who follow Elsie Archer's suggestions should find themselves better prepared to adapt themselves to their environment and be happier within themselves."—RUBY HURLEY, *Regional Secretary, National Association for the Advancement of Colored People*

"Elsie Archer has approached the problems girls face with personal interest and deep understanding. The girls in Mrs. Archer's classes here leave with a deeper sense of self-confidence, poise and dignity, and are better able to get along in all segments of society."—MARY L. GIBSON, *Director, Gibson School of Charm, New York City*

"*Let's Face It* has greatly aided the development of a healthy self-image among our girls....Orchids to Elsie Archer for conceiving this volume which provides information on grooming, poise, personality, clothing selection, complexion care, and many other topics so important to the young girl."—HORTENSE WILLIAMS GRAY, *Dean of Girls, William M. Raines High School, Jacksonville, Florida*

"*Let's Face It* serves as a guide for young people of all economical levels to discover beauty, poise, and a deeper self-understanding, so important in the midst of rapid social changes taking place in today's society. It has become a necessary tool in my department."—JACQUELINE WELLINGTON-MOORE, *Grooming Teacher and Liaison Worker, Department of Social Services, New York City*

LET'S FACE IT

The Guide to Good Grooming
for Girls of Color

Elsie Archer

REVISED EDITION

J. B. Lippincott Company

PHILADELPHIA AND NEW YORK

Contents

LET'S
FACE IT

I

Facing the Facts

START WITH YOU

If you're like most girls your age, you've been doing some serious thinking. But the big problem is that your thoughts change from day to day, and this is upsetting. But more disturbing than that is that your thoughts always turn to YOU!

Don't let this bother you. It's only natural that you start, now, to give serious thought to yourself. YOU as you are today . . . and YOU as you want to be later on. There is a time for everything and things must be done on time. TODAY is the time for you to start thinking about your aims, your ambitions and your goals.

If you're serious . . . really serious . . . and want to do something about you and your future, you've taken your first big step. Just taking time out to read this book indicates that you mean business. So if this is the way it is with you, you might as well settle down and get started. Where to start, is another problem. It need not be! How about starting with you? Your age doesn't matter when it comes to facing up to the facts about you. The younger you are, the better.

PICTURE YOUR FUTURE

Every girl has a very clear picture, in her mind, how she wants to look today and all the days to follow. There's nothing to worry about if you're not satisfied with yourself as you are today. Most girls aren't. But don't just sit there, quietly complaining to yourself about all the things that displease you: do something about them.

This sounds easy but you know darn well it isn't. How can it be, when you don't even know where to begin and just what changes to make? Your thoughts are running away with you. One day you want to look one way and the next day the picture of you has changed completely. You know, for sure, something must be dreadfully wrong with you for feeling this way. You were satisfied with yourself before. But now, everything is wrong . . . all wrong!

Did it ever occur to you that your little girl days are gone, and now you're beginning to feel like a real important person? You are! Important to your family, your friends and important to all those that come in contact with you. But more than that, you must be important to yourself. The picture you have of yourself and your future need not be only a dream. You can make it real. But before you do, you must believe in yourself . . . have faith in yourself and the things you do, and the changes you want to make will come easy.

Speaking of importance, it might make you feel better if you knew that back in 1966 the United States Department of Commerce counted 815,000 non-white girls between fifteen and nineteen years old. You may have been in that number. If not, you will be when they come around to take the count the next time. But this is how important you are.

Where do you find yourself, whether you were in that count or not? Smack dab in the middle of adolescence and adulthood. What happened? How did you get here so quickly? What happened to those little girl days? One day, there you were with arms and legs that just seemed to be dangling and not belonging to the rest of your body. You just seemed to shoot up like a weed, or it looked as if you didn't grow at all. At least not in the right direction. If, today, you find yourself bulging at the seams with too much fat, you certainly don't want to be called "fatso" for the rest of your life. Neither do you want to drag around like a sack of skeleton bones that never seem to have enough flesh to cover them. And on the other hand, you might be thinking you're O.K. just as you are and you couldn't care less about being any better. Which ever way it is with you, changes are in order. Even if you think you're at your best, you can always be better.

MAKE A PLAN

It can be fun working out a plan for a new you. It will be even more fun when you see changes taking place each and every day. Once you get started, you can't turn back. You wouldn't do this to yourself. Now is the time for you to stand on your own two feet and make plans and decisions for yourself. You have a long way to go, and much work to do. Start now!

You know the most important thing staring you in the face is YOUR LIFE! So you concentrate on just that. You know, because your common sense tells you so, that your life will be what you make it. You know that life offers you, a non-white teen-ager, more today than ever before. You know that your life will be as successful as you will want to make it. You know that the profits are plentiful, but the gain will depend on how much of you goes into it. You know that now is the time to start your investment for the future. That investment is YOU.

You're on your own. There's lots of work to be done. All of it must be done by you. Your parents, your family and friends can only encourage you and guide you, but you must do the work. The hopes of young girls your age are high. One day you want to be this, the next day something else. Somewhere in between you wonder if you really have what it takes to accomplish these hopes, and if you can make your dreams come true.

If you're not sure you can find the answer . . . take a look. Look at yourself in a mirror, and you'll find the answer right there. If you care enough about yourself and your future, you can and will accomplish these dreams and many, many more. You can have all in life that you want. It's true, you may never be honored for a great medical discovery, you may never be an olympic champion, never swim the Atlantic, never win a beauty contest nor be Miss America, never be one of Hollywood's greatest stars, never see your name in bright lights on Broadway and never the first girl astronaut. Yes, all these things may seem way out of your reach. But if you work at developing into the kind of individual you want to be, facing each day with an attitude that will help you get the most out of that day . . . another kind of success can be yours.

YOUR LUCKY DAY

Yes, all this can be fun—if you make it that way. You are a very lucky girl. Lucky to be born in this fantastic world. With so many new products created just for you and other girls your age, it will be fun just to use them and look for the results. Some of these things work so quickly, it almost seems like a miracle. And even though you know that miracles don't exist, it will be great fun anyway just knowing you had a hand in the changes. Nothing works without your help. When a new you slowly and clearly comes to light, what a thrill it will be. But the added joy comes when others take notice of these changes and tell you so. Then you know it's all worthwhile.

KNOW YOURSELF

It may seem that you're headed into a selfish program, even if it is worthwhile. You are! For a short period, anyway. You must spend every moment getting to know yourself. Know what you are and what you want to be. Know what you like and what you don't. And above all, know what you believe in and those things you disagree with.

There's no time for fooling around. Start at once! You won't be sorry. You're smart to do this. Most girls want to but not too many do. The clever girl starts early in her life, as you're doing. Those not-so-clever will go through life, day in and day out, dreaming and wishing for something that could have been hers if she had only done something about working for it. But you have cut out the day dreaming and wishful thinking. You want to know what life expects of you and what you're to expect of it. This is your reason for taking a closer look at yourself and wanting to do something about it.

You've learned so much from your parents, but you want to learn more. You want to learn more about your body . . . how to shape and form it correctly and beautifully. You want to learn how to care for it and keep it clean and feminine. You want to learn more about your hair . . . how to give it better care . . . how to keep it styled appropriately and attractively. You want to know more about your skin and some of the do-it-yourself tricks to help keep it clean, clear and lovely. You know, already, that the color of your skin is important. Regardless how light or how dark it is, it is important to you. You want to know how to make it make you the beauty you want to be.

You realize the fortune you have in healthy teeth, attractive hands and pretty feet. All these are your most valuable tools; if any one of them is neglected you will not and cannot make that "band-box" clean-as-a-whistle appearance expected of you.

WHAT MAKES YOU TICK

Then you'll want to learn what makes you tick . . . why you're the way you are . . . why you do and say the things you do. You will want to know more about developing a pleasing personality . . . the right attitude toward yourself, your family and your life. You are wondering about your friends . . . girl friends and, more importantly, boy friends. You're wondering why you do or do not have them. You know, in addition to all these very important facts, your future progress will also depend on the way you dress (with or without a budget), the way you act, the way you talk, walk, sit and stand . . . and you want to learn how to improve each.

You know how useful spare time can be. Your future depends on it, if you use it wisely. You want to learn how to take better advantage of it. You want every moment of every day to count because you know that this will make you as you want to be. An unforgettable, lovely you. A charming, more attractive you. A you that will be happy. A you that is well on the road to a successful future. This is a big job. It is your job. Your full responsibility.

THERE'S ENOUGH TIME

This is a job you can't cheat on. There's no doing a little today and coming back weeks later expecting to take up where you left off. You may be thinking, this is going to take too much time, and you haven't got this kind of time to spare. But there is enough time. The seconds, the minutes and the hours in each day don't change. There's no more or no less in each day for you. A day is as long for you as it is for all other girls your age. You will find the time to get every job done, but it's up to you to put your time to good use and make every moment count.

You either rearrange your time schedule to fit a self-improvement program into your life, or you can forget it. . . . now! The smart girls know how necessary this is to their future. They want to be in the swim of things . . . where the action is . . . doing things . . . things that count. And why shouldn't you? You know more about yourself than anyone, and what you don't know, you'll soon find out. You will know where improvement is needed. The important thing to know is that a little time each day spent on improving yourself will help correct figure faults, personality defects and facial ugliness.

HELP YOURSELF TO SUCCESS

This book will not help you mechanically prepare for your future. It will, with your determination and your hard work, help you to become more personable, more attractive, and it will help you to become a girl who will not be left on the side lines. It will help you to be someone who is loved and wanted, and one who will be accepted wherever you are and wherever you go.

If you're smart, and I know you are, you don't have to be told you're living in a world of opportunity. Help yourself to it. If you're serious about getting this job done, don't let anything stand in your way . . . and success will be yours. Success is wanting something out of life and happiness is making sure you work to get it.

Take the wise words of John Milton, along the way with you:

> Accuse not Nature, she hath done her part;
> do thou but thine

With these facts tucked under your belt, you will not fail. Work seriously and the job will be fun. The facts are here. The rest is up to you. Good luck.

2

You and Your Health

When you decide to settle down, the days ahead will be filled with excitement, enthusiasm and joy. The changes will be slow, at first. But if you watch closely, they will take place right before your eyes. Be patient! Nothing worthwhile can be done in a hurry.

The picture of you should be clearly outlined in your mind. What you want to be, how you want to look is stamped right there. Your dreams, your hopes locked in tight, hidden from the rest of the world, and nobody has the key but you. If you don't want to be disappointed, don't set your hopes too high. Don't plan for the impossible. Be sensible. Don't flatter yourself. Don't overrate yourself. If the picture of you is real, your plans for a personal development program will be easy.

Making a plan is one thing, but following it is something else. Don't try to squeeze too many things into one day. You know what you have to do, with school and homework and other tasks. Putting too many things into one day will find you somewhere between here and there, out of strength, no energy, no interest and giving up forever. Stick with it, and you'll be proud when your plan begins to pay off. It will, if you organize it properly.

Things may not run too smoothly, at first. On some days, you might wonder if it's all worth it. It is! Don't let discouragement slip in. It will only slow up your progress. Everyone wants to make changes. Everyone wants to improve. In this day of modern progress changes are necessary. You must make them to measure up to the standards set up for you. That is if you want a big hunk of the success that is out there waiting for you.

LOOK AT A HEALTHY YOU

A good starting place is with your health. It is your foundation for beauty. It comes first! Good health is the assurance of a beautiful you.

Not enough sleep, the wrong foods, not going to the bathroom everyday, can be just a few of the reasons for a bedraggled, lifeless you. Who needs this? Life can be beautiful. But you must be healthy to appreciate it. It's impossible for you to look your prettiest, if your health is not letter perfect.

How much do you really know about your health? Up to now, you depended on your family or some other adult to be sure your health was what it should have been. That was great. Then you had nothing to worry about. They either told you when to get a checkup from the doctor, or they took you by the hand and led you there. No more of that for you. You're a big girl now. You can do these things for yourself from now on.

YOUR FRIEND — THE DOCTOR

The first big step into your new self-improvement plan is a trip to the doctor. One that you know personally, or the one from the school clinic or the hospital clinic near you. He can help you solve so many problems. Your skin, your hair, poor sleeping habits and lack of appetite can develop into major health problems. The doctor, first off the bat, can help you with them. There is no reason to be afraid. Don't let his white uniform frighten you. The doctor can and will be one of your best friends. Believe me, you need a friend like him.

Relax and feel free to question him about your health. He will welcome the chance to answer your questions. He will be happy to know you're that interested in yourself. Clearing up some of your questions will help you to know better the function of your organs and their relation to the function of the rest of your body. You may be bashful and a little uneasy about discussing your body changes, your menstruation periods or even sex with your parents. You don't have to feel this way at all with the doctor. When you're with him, open up and discuss any of these subjects freely with him. Even if it's sex you want to know more about, here is the place to discuss it. That is if you haven't already done so with your parents. It is much better for you to understand clearly the beauty of sex relations now and the dangers of sex before you are married. It is advisable to get professional information and your doctor is the best person to ask.

THE SUBJECT OF SEX

Sex is an important subject, demanding important decisions. This is just one of the reasons that it is no longer a hidden subject. It can and is being discussed openly and freely. Magazine and newspaper articles, film strips and pamphlets all report the true facts. It is even being discussed in schools from the first grade up. You take it from there and give it the importance it deserves and make your own decisions.

If you're having a discussion about sex with the doctor, he may want to ask you questions. Don't be ashamed to answer them. This is one of the many places where honesty pays off. You may not realize it, but the doctor knows when you're not telling the truth.

You can tell him everything about you. Your health record is kept in a safe place, for no other eyes to see. All private details are tucked carefully away in his professional mind. The doctor cannot afford to discuss "you" with others. His reputation is at stake. He must protect it.

MAKE FREQUENT TRIPS

Regular trips to the doctor's office will help you recognize any unhealthy habits in your everyday living. The healthy ones you can't help but see. Neglected minor aches and pains may develop into major ones later on. Any unusual developments in your health habits need the advice of your doctor. Every part of your body—your feet, your eyes, ears, nose, your skin and your teeth—can be treated by individuals specializing in these particular body parts. If special treatment is necessary, your regular physician will direct you to these specialists. With things as they are today, everyone can afford "special" medical care.

If doctors make you nervous, at least discuss unusual health signs with your mother or someone older than yourself. You will find they know more about these things than you think they do. Take advantage of their years of experience. Don't be a know-it-all about your health. It can be dangerous!

PILLS CAN BE DANGEROUS

Whatever you do, don't be pill happy! The vitamin pill is one of the greatest things that ever happened to medical science, but too many of us think a little pastel-coated pill can cure anything and everything. Too many people turn too quickly to the aid of vitamin pills, rather than to the doctor. The corner drugstore is overstocked with pills, every color, every shape and size. My advice to you is to leave them right where they are unless your doctor prescribes them for you. Let's not misunderstand: vitamins taken properly can be helpful. But before you "buy and try" without knowing just what it is you're buying, consult your physician. If your visits to him have been regular, he will be familiar with your medical needs. Take his advice. Follow his directions.

SLEEP MAKES A HEALTHY YOU

Do you know how important sleep is to good health and beauty? If you get enough of it, it is the greatest beauty formula there is. Your good looks are hurt if you're not getting plenty of it. Going without eight hours or so of sleep may not show up in your face right now, but it will sooner or later. If you think you can cut down on the amount you get each night, and hope to make up for it later on, you're mistaken. If you don't believe it, just try it and see for yourself what happens to your health and to your beauty. Many girls require as much as nine to ten hours each night. But the average, healthy young girl must get a full eight hours and every night.

In this space age when everything, but everything, is done in a hurry, you're bound to be tired, tense and beat. Some nights it's not easy for you to unwind and relax. Heavy school assignments, hour long end-of-term examinations, and perhaps a heavy work load after school leaves you nervous and tense. With a schedule like this, how can you avoid being tense and tired? But you can't afford to let school work and examinations interfere with your nervous system and sleep. You must get enough sleep so your thinking facilities are in good working order.

If you seek professional help, the doctor may advise you to get more than your regular amount of sleep. He may even suggest rest periods during the day. This can restore normal health quicker than any medicine your druggist has to offer. Proper rest and enough sleep helps you to operate better. Sleep helps speed up the function of your brain. It helps you overcome tiredness, tension and body strain. It makes you feel more like doing things. Powder and paint will not cover up lack-of-sleep signs. Lines appear around your eyes and the glow of color disappears from your complexion. Your body movements slow down and your sunny disposition turns sour.

We are not likely to ever forget the beauty of Miss Lena Horne, the proud possessor of blemish-free skin. Over a period of years, her skin is still free of lines and wrinkles. Her complexion glows like the golden sunlight and her skin is firm, healthy, radiant and truly beautiful. Without a doubt, sleep has been her keynote to a beautiful success —the success of charm, the success of poise and a pleasing personality and of feminine loveliness.

Speaking of facial beauty, don't forget the lively look of The Supremes. Even though much younger in age, they have had to map out a routine to fit their popularity. The look of healthy smooth skin comes right through the heavy use of "on-stage" make up. They have not allowed an overtime working schedule to interfere with their sleep-for-beauty formula. It has made these three as beautiful, slim and elegant as the swingy pop tunes they sing. Such beauty is not "push button magic." Each of these girls long ago realized that sleep was the important helper up the ladder of beauty success.

A change in your sleep schedule should only happen

occasionally, say on weekends. If you're up a little later on Friday or Saturday nights, make up for it on the following morning. It's the loss of sleep, night after night that does the injury to both health and beauty.

TAKE A BREAK

A break in regular routine is always a help. Take short rest periods, if your daily program is heavy and strenuous. Getting away from any regular routine, even for a minute or two, eases the mental strain. A few minutes of complete quiet, saying and doing nothing, can also be effective. Clear your mind of everything. Just float away into another world for a few minutes. When you come back to earth again, fresh thoughts will flow smoothly and you'll feel like a brand new girl.

If you're one of the lucky ones who goes out on dates, this is a sure way of putting you at your best. Not only will you be a pleasure to be with, you just might be asked out again.

If getting away from it all doesn't do the trick, and you are tired and run-down most of the time, this is serious. It's even more serious if loss of weight accompanies this feeling. You can't afford to overlook persistent headaches and stomach pains. They might be danger signals telling you that something is wrong.

SPARKLING EYES

How lucky you are to have your eyes, and more so if they're in good working order. Protect them from too much strain. You will have headaches and pain if the light is bad where you study and read. It's good to have your eyes checked professionally. This check may be done at your school.

An occasional eyewash is known to put sparkle back

into tired eyes that have worked overtime. Boric acid solution is a good eye-brightener. Cotton pads wet with witch hazel or any eye solution is another good way to relieve tired eyes. Try either—it is a soothing way to encourage you to relax—not just your eyes, but your entire body.

REGULAR ROUTINE

Poor elimination is another sure cause of headaches. Staying in bed five or ten minutes longer in the mornings cuts down on bathroom time. This is time that you need to get yourself going in the morning. A hop-skip-jump-and-run-program with no time for relaxed elimination is no way to start your day. Constipation is another robber of pep and strength. Constipation can destroy your whole day. If you miss the bathroom routine one day, it's hard to get back on the track the next. Don't depend on medicine to keep you "regular." Just rearranging your daily program may be the only help you need. Cheating on time to relieve this waste matter is cheating on your health. Watch the food you eat. The right foods will encourage elimination. Steady constipation with no relief must be discussed with the doctor. He probably is the only one to take you out of your discomfort.

A constant run of colds leaves you weak and headachy. One cold after the other can be dangerous to your health. Simple colds, that appear too often, are "front men" for something more serious to follow. A lingering cough that follows a cold is risky. You are taking your life in your hands when you allow these signs to go unnoticed. Cold tablets and cough syrup bought over the drug counter are dangerous unless they have been prescribed for you professionally.

Taking medicine for every little thing that goes wrong will do a good job of tangling and twisting your nervous system. You're much too young to start complaining of "nerves." Leave that bad habit for those who don't know any better. Keep your body in a normal healthy state by keeping it clean . . . inside and out. Correct your bad eating and sleeping habits, make sure your meals are properly balanced (see Chapter 4) and include those foods that are necessary to good health. Get as much sunshine and exercise as your schedule will allow and above all see your doctor when you know it is necessary.

3

This Is Your Body

The very first item on your good grooming program is cleanliness . . . clean all the way, from top to toe. Start with your body.

No matter how you feel about your body today, that feeling will change later on. This is where the real fun begins.

START WITH A BATH

For a successful beauty plan, start with a bath. This is so very important. Taking a bath is not as simple as you may think. Would you believe that statistics show that eight and a half million American homes are without private bath or shower? Did it ever occur to you that so many people were without modern bathing facilities? If your bathroom is fully equipped with everything to work with, you're lucky!

Isn't it a good feeling to know that you no longer have to be "hit over the head" or "screamed at" to take a bath? Now you realize how good a bath is for you. A bath does wonderful things for you and your body. It lifts your morale, and gives you self-confidence. When you're clean . . . really clean . . . you want to be "on the scene" doing things, being a part of the action.

The time of day for taking a bath doesn't matter. Take it when it's convenient for you. But bathing every single day is important. Whether it's in a bathtub, out of a wash basin or under the shower is of no consequence. Just so your body is clean is what counts the most. A tub bath, at night when there's not so much bathroom traffic might be a good arrangement. If, on the other hand, you're a sleepy-head and need something to put you on your feet in the morning, a bath is a great eye-opener. It removes that sleepy, lazy, sluggish feeling. You may even prefer bathing when you come in from school or work when you can have the bathroom all to yourself. This way you don't have to hurry along for the next person waiting in line. Whenever and whatever, just don't let anything interfere with your bathing routine. Enough time must be given for self-satisfying results. A "quickie" bath, with your wash cloth splashing around in "catch as catch can" fashion, will not give you the clean skin you'll be happy with. One of those in-the-tub-out-again baths is no good either. There is just no possible way for you to get clean this way. Head-to-toe scrubbing is the only way.

ONE A DAY

There is no excuse for a slip-shod cleaning routine. Getting into a bathtub of warm water is nice, if it's available. Even if your home is without a good supply of hot running water, you can still give your body the necessary daily scrubbing, even if it means heating a kettle of water on the kitchen stove. The water only does half the job. The soap contains the cleaning power. The energy you put into it and the amount of soap you use is what works successfully. It will only work, however, if every inch of your body is scrubbed clean . . . every day.

Don't let anything sway you from this everday routine. It's an old belief that a bath once or twice a week keeps you clean enough. Girls your age are more active today. They're doing more things. Don't deprive yourself of this cleaning pleasure.

You might remember, from your history books, the story of Benjamin Franklin and his bathing habits. He was the first to bring a formal bathtub into this country, so the story goes. His bathtub was an unusually funny sight. That it was made of tin and shaped like a shoe is enough to stop you right there. There was not too much water around and that presented the first problem. He had to make his own soap. There's a second problem. The water brought in from the nearby streams or wells was heated on the stove and taken to his shoe-like bathtub in small vessels. Just think of the time this must have taken. Who would want to go through this every day? Naturally he was restricted to once-a-week bathing, so would you if you had been born back in those days. But today, the modern up-to-date American way of keeping your body clean and healthy is everyday bathing, all year 'round. It is ridiculous to think you can let up on body cleanliness during the cold winter months.

It is also ridiculous to think that wintertime baths cause colds and encourage muscle soreness and body pains. It may be necessary to change the time of your daily baths. Instead of taking a morning bath and expose your body to the cold weather, switch to taking it at night.

Your body has two or three million oil glands. These glands throw off some oil each day, which meets up with the surface dirt and dust. This mixture leaves a film of dirt that you can't see too well on the top of the skin, all during the year. The season has nothing at all to do with it. Naturally, during the hot weather, the film of dirt and perspiration is apt to be more plentiful, and baths must be more frequent.

MAKE EACH MINUTE COUNT

Even if you take several baths a day, a good bath requires time. Make each minute count and give every area the attention that is needed. Your ears, a delicate part of your body, will expect gentle cleaning, inside and out. Gouging and digging too deep will injure the delicate membranes. Take it easy! Forgetting your neck is an unpardonable sin. Keep it clean like your face. They must look as if they belong together.

Your back can stand a little attention, too. Keep it as smooth and clean as your face and neck. If you skip over it now, you'll be sorry when summer comes along. Daily scrubbing will keep it smooth and soft and free of pimples and ugly bumps. If you haven't already done so, introduce yourself to one of those long-handled back brushes. With a generous amount of soap and water, the firm bristles will ease away dead surface skin and loosen blackheads in hard-to-reach spots. A gentle back and forth motion is all that is required. After a good scrubbing, a healthy application of oil or body lotion will keep your skin smooth and lovely, all ready for low cut dresses and skimpy bathing suits.

Discolored heels and darkened elbows require particular attention. Chapters Eight and Nine will help you with each when you want to care for them individually. Spend more time on both places during your bath, and the "private" attention care will take less time.

Make sure all the soap is removed after each bathing

session. Soap left on your body dries up, leaving a scaley surface. For a real treat and a thorough rinsing, get under the shower. Another sure trick is rinsing off with a sponge and just as enjoyable. When the fun is all over, dry thoroughly.

BATH OILS AND BUBBLES

There should not be any set limit on the number of baths you take daily. In most places, water is free; you don't have to be stingy with bathing. One bath is good, but if a good reason presents itself, give yourself an extra treat and take two. That second bath, the one just before a date, could be the time to add a luxury item just to break your bathing routine. Highly scented bath crystals, pastel-colored bubble beads, bath oils, bath perfumes or any one of your favorite scents are helpmates in making your bath more enjoyable. A bubble bath is loads of fun and gives you a feeling of luxury as you nestle under the sweet warm bubbles. This is a wonderful way to soak up all the good things that happened during the day. It gives you time to think about the enjoyment that faces you.

BATH TOWELS AND WASH CLOTHES

Keep an eagle eye on all your bathing equipment and especially your washcloth and bath towel. For the short time you're using them, they're your own private property. Keep them clean. The towels that touch your body and.face must not carry germs. It's such a good feeling when your bathing gear has a clean, fresh smell. If there are little ones around that are likely to meddle with your things, keep your "personals" out of reach of dirty little hands and fingers. Find a special place for them, and they will be clean when you need them again.

SELECT SOAPS FOR BODY SMOOTHNESS

It has been said that non-white, dark skins dry out more quickly than others. Whether this is true or not, one thing we do know is that strong, harsh soap will leave any skin hard and dry, regardless of color. The exact same thing can happen to the skin from winter cold or summer sun. All this dryness can be smoothed away with an over-all lubrication job. Play it safe and select a soap with an oil base for skin protection. When dryness occurs, for whatever reasons, a resupply of oil is needed. After each bath, try a good rubdown with body lotion or oil. Apply just enough to give an over-all softness and smoothness to your entire body. It need not be fancy or expensive. Baby oil or lotion is as good as anything I know. It's economical too! Both can be purchased in the five and dime store.

BODY OIL AND LOTION

Diahann Carroll sends you a message about how she takes care of body-dryness. Diahann, no longer a teen-ager, but the mother of a little girl of her own, has a body that is as soft, silky and as polished as the songs she sings. Strangely enough, she did not always have this body smoothness. But believe it or not, Diahann shakes up equal portions each of oil and lotion, making a rich, fluffy, cream-like body lotion. Diahann says, "A singing career demands more than a good voice. Strong theatrical spotlights require a complexion, from head to toe, that glows with a healthy firm smoothness. Bright lights reveal personal neglect," she reveals. "My skin has always been excessively dry and the combination of the baby lotion and oil has worked wonders for me. It adds a bright gleam and a new body sparkle to my dry parched skin. I use it 'all over' after each bath, and on some days they add up to three when my schedule is heavy." Shake up a supply for yourself. For a beginning, buy the small size of each . . . the lotion and the oil. Pour the contents into a larger bottle and shake until you get the just right creamy smooth spread-on look. It will give your body a gentle smoothness, and at the same time help restore the shortage of oil missing from your skin. It's certainly worth a try. And remember, if it's good enough for a baby's skin (and Diahann Carroll's), what harm can it do to yours?

BATHE IN OIL

When time permits, free your body of the dull, ashen-gray coating with an oil bath. Your body will truly radiate when it's over. Run half the amount of water you generally put into the bathtub. Oil your body from top to toe, face included. Slip into the tub. Let the water run slowly, hot as you can take it, until you feel you're completely relaxed and the tub is full. Recline and relax! (Don't go to sleep; you may never come out alive, if you do!) The steam co-operates with the oil. It digs the dirt from the pores, softens up all the old rough skin and eases blackheads right up to the surface of the skin. Step out! Wrap yourself in your bath towel. Once that water is out, refill your tub with warm water. This time soap and scrub as you usually do. When you're all rinsed and dried, pat your favorite cologne over your body or dust it with your fragrant body powder. You have no idea how good this will make you feel until you've tried it. If your skin is excessively dry, an oil bath is the best remedy. Skin dryness shows up more on dark-toned skins, adding more importance to skin lubrication. The steam and oil will leave your body delightfully soft, smooth as silk and your skin will reveal a deep-down cleanliness.

BODY ODOR AND PERSPIRATION

There may be little you can do about perspiration but you can't make excuses for body odor.

You perspire! You have to! Your health requires it! You may not perspire more than other girls your age, or maybe not as much, but perspiration is there. Even right after your bath, a slight dampness is present under your arms and other areas where hair growth is prevalent. This normal perspiration has a very faint odor, if any at all. But when it meets up with skin-surface dust and oil this is when trouble starts, if ignored. This is why it is so essential to keep your body clean so that unpleasant odors can be kept down to a minimum. But you can't rely on the cleaning power of your soap and the effectiveness of your bath oil, the sweetness of your cologne or dusting powder to last forever. Did you know that you have your own individual body odor? One that is not unpleasant, but just you. Everyone has! You don't notice this natural odor; your nostrils have become accustomed to it, one of the reasons why it takes you so long to notice any unpleasantness. This is why deodorants are so important to your daily personal care plan.

Your age doesn't make the slightest difference when it comes to using a deodorant. If perspiration is there, then it's your job to keep down strong unpleasant body odors. Perspiration and body odors show up early for many girls. Others don't notice perspiration at all, until they are way up in their teens. The main thing is not to let it go by unnoticed. Don't take chances! You need assistance to control your perspiration. There are all types of deodorants on the market that will help you with this problem.

You might like to try the smooth cream-type or the easy roll-on from the bottle, or the cooling and refreshing sensation of a spray. It's a good idea to test your choice in the bend of your arm, to prove any irritation. Your skin may be sensitive to any irritating chemicals. Whatever your selection, it must give you the best service. If your budget will not allow for such a purchase, a temporary remedy is powdering on plain baking soda, found right in your kitchen cupboard. The soda will cut down perspiration and its odor until you can do better.

DON'T TAKE CHANCES

An internal disorder could be one of the reasons for an excessively strong body odor. Menstruation is another reason for strong body odors. Extreme care must be taken at this time every month. During this period, your body tosses off accumulated waste matter, and it comes through all body channels. More than likely, body odors will be stronger. Extra precaution is advisable. Even during this time of the month, you want to retain your feminine charm. Again, make doubly sure your body is carefully cleaned each day. A bath is very necessary. It need not be a "sit in" bath. Your doctor will tell you it is not harmful. Change your sanitary pads or tampons several times a day. They carry unpleasant odors if they are not fresh and clean. Use your talcum powder freely. Keep sweet-smelling by patting a little between your legs and on your sanitary pad if necessary.

UNWANTED HAIR

In many parts of the world, there are still girls who because of customs do not know how to get rid of hair growing under the arms and on the legs. Wherever you are, smooth arm pits and legs are an accepted part of good grooming.

Let's face it, a body beautiful must be one that is smooth and clean all the way. What can be more unattractive than a thick patch of hair growing under your arms, when your arms are bare and your dress is without sleeves? This gives one the impression that you are not clean. A dark patch of hair in your armpits can spoil your costume no matter how beautiful or expensive. When unwanted hair has been removed, you feel clean all the way. The time to start removing this hair is when it's definitely noticeable and the growth is heavy. If just a fuzz appears, the removal job can wait for a while. If the growth is heavy, a razor or depilatory cream is needed. A thick growth of hair on your legs is ugly, unsightly and unfeminine, too.

RAZORS

The razor method rates high on the popularity list. Manufacturers have produced razors all sizes and shapes to help you with your feminine loveliness. These razors are made especially for feminine use. They are curved to fit the groove under your arm or shaped to follow the contour of your leg. Some of these new razors don't require a lather; read the directions. The hair is most effectively removed by running the razor in the opposite direction from which the hair grows. Hold off a while before applying a deodorant. It might sting and burn. The directions on the deodorant will instruct you how long you should wait.

CREAMS

For absolute protection and safety, and if you have the time, try a depilatory cream. These hair-removing creams contain strong chemicals that penetrate below the surface of the skin and break the hair off there. This method will take a little longer, but the hair doesn't grow back as quickly. The cream is applied to the area where the hair is growing and remains there, to dry, for ten or twelve minutes, according to the directions. Once the cream has had sufficient time to dry, it is washed away with warm clear water and the hair goes along with it. This leaves a clean smooth skin and the hair has been removed without danger.

OTHER REMOVAL METHODS

You might try a hair-removing glove. This method is easy and simple to use if a fine fuzz is appearing for the first time. The sandpapery part that is rubbed on the skin where the hair grows might be irritating if the hair growth is too thick. This can be a good "in-between" treatment, cleaning up the reappearance of hair between shaving. There are also nice-smelling lotions that do a good job. Try any one of them; just make sure you read the directions and follow them as they are printed. They are put there for your protection and this is the only way you will get good results.

4

Shaping Your Body

After taking one look at your body, if you think this whole beauty program is hopeless, you've got another thought coming. If the picture of you is bad, shaping it up in places, or all over, will make it look better. Shaping and molding your body, today, can be the beginning of body perfection from now on.

Exercises make your body limber. They keep you graceful and your muscles tight and firm. Long after your teen years daily exercises will be your greatest aid in keeping your body flat and firm in the right places. But more important, they work up the circulation and keep you from feeling stiff and awkward.

You can actually change the shape of your body to one that is either slimmer or fuller. If this is the case, why not do something about the shape of yours now?

TAKE A LOOK

The easy way to start is to take a good look, in a full length mirror. The truth is right there before you. Facing up to the truth about yourself is not easy, but the truth about your body and its shape is there. Are you popping out in the wrong places or is there barely enough flesh to cover you? Don't think this picture of you will change just by concealing your figure problems with clothes. It is true, clothes are sometimes known as "shape makers," but when you know the real truth about what's going on underneath, that's another story. You're real lucky, anyhow, if you can find clothes that will cover all your figure problems. Generally clothes don't. They only help. When you're dressed, you may think you look pretty groovy. Your mind may tell you one thing, but your mirror will not lie to you. You may just as well face up to the truth now and then do something about it. When beach time rolls around, you'll have a figure that's "out of sight," and there will be no need to hide under a tent.

ARE THE POUNDS STACKED UP IN YOUR FAVOR?

You may be one of those girls who has nothing to worry about, figurewise. If you think you're stacked up in the right places, stay that way. But don't let it go to your head. If you're lucky and careful, keeping in shape will be easy for you. Watch your diet, check your health and get enough exercise . . . every day. Nothing pleases a guy more than a "well stacked" swinging female. You feel even better when the girls look at you admiringly and with envy.

Now on the other hand, you might not be so lucky. If you're seriously out of shape and too much fat has given you no shape at all, you really have a job to do. Nobody, but nobody, wants to be fat. Being overweight is bad for your health and can give you a grumpy, ugly disposition. Any smart girl, concerned about her appearance, worries when fat begins to spread. Take it from me, you'll get fatter and fatter, if you don't check it . . . NOW!

If you're still quite young and baby fat makes you look more square than round, you have just as much work to do as the girl older than you. Taking baby fat for granted and eating everything you get your hands on only makes a chubby figure rounder and fatter. The "I'll grow out of it" attitude has its good and bad points. Maybe you will and maybe you won't! Don't gamble! You can't afford it! This is where fat begins and this is where it will stay, for the rest of your natural life, unless you stop it now!

You must be reasonable and sensible when it comes to slicing off the pounds. Four or five pounds in one direction or the other is not such a big job. But ten or fifteen pounds is something to worry about.

LOSING WEIGHT

An excessive amount of weight loss requires medical guidance. Let the professional tell you how many of these pounds you can lose for your particular body build and remain healthy. Let someone that knows more about these things than you give you the hard, cold figure facts. They will tell you what to gain or lose. You may think you're too fat, but maybe you're just right . . . from a health standpoint. Figure fixing can be dangerous. The state of your health may require you to carry a few extra pounds. But if you're just plain fat, then your figure needs adjusting.

THE WRONG FOODS

How did you get fat, anyway? Your list of reasons is probably long. The most popular weight-builder is overeating. This is the one reason we are most familiar with. Any intelligent person knows that you're bound to get fat if you stuff yourself with all the wrong foods. Gooey sweets and desserts piled "a mile high" with whipped cream and ice cream will certainly add extra pounds if you over-do. Don't pay any attention to those that tell you you're fat because your family is. If they are, and you are too, you've just picked up all their wrong eating habits. Starches, rich foods cooked and seasoned with fat meat, grease and bacon will put pounds on you quicker than you can get through the day.

HOW YOU GOT THAT WAY

An out-of-order thyroid gland is a second reason for gaining weight. Individual emotional problems can be another. Family problems and personal worry that rest heavily on your shoulders cause emotional strain. Most young girls turn to eating for mental relief. They think the only way to comfort is to nibble. We all have a strong desire to eat, but this desire grows stronger when signs of stress and strain appear . . . and the wrong foods always seem to be in easy reach.

Girls, young and old, are unhappy when they're fat . . . really fat. They generally find themselves pulling away from the group. They are not "in there" doing things. They are alone. Always alone! Being fat takes away your pep. You just never have enough energy to keep up with what's happening. You puff and you blow. You become lazy and sluggish; consequently, you have so much more time to eat. And you get fatter, and fatter and fatter.

I've heard some girls say that the color of their skin is one of the reasons they were pushed out of the swing of things. With this lame excuse they eat to fill up the vacancy in their lives. This is kind of silly, when you know you're the only one to suffer for such thoughts

Whom are you hurting? No one but yourself! The color of your skin has nothing to do with being overweight. But since we're on the subject, the color of your skin has never been more important than it is today. Being fat need not mean complete disaster for you, but the trimmer and more attractive you can make yourself, the better it will be for you in the long run.

DO SOMETHING ABOUT IT

Even though such thoughts can create mental disorders, again you may need medical help to overcome some of these problems, that is, if you don't have enough willpower of your own. If you're overweight, just losing some of the extra pounds and inches will do much for you. Once you start to slim down, just a pound or two will make you feel better immediately. You begin to look like a new person. You discover a new feminine charm. Your clothes look more attractive on you. You have a different outlook on life. You know your chances are greater with a body that seems to "fit in" wherever you are.

You know all these things arc true, and you honestly want to do something about re-shaping your figure, but you don't like the idea of giving up all the good things you like to eat. Having to live with a tasteless diet is not for you. You don't like the idea of counting and weighing everything you eat. You just can't see yourself walking around with a calorie chart tucked under your nose twenty-four hours a day. You just can't put yourself through this torture, even if it docs mean a neat, trim figure. Would you believe you don't have to do any of these things to have a near-new figure?

GIVING UP THE GOODIES

Unless your doctor puts you on a carefully planned diet, there is no reason for you to give up the foods you like.

If you're overweight, your approach to eating must be sensible and serious. Get three full meals into your daily schedule. Skipping meals, especially breakfast, will not help you lose weight. For active young girls, skipping meals only gives you a better appetite when the next meal rolls around. To keep in shape and in good health, breakfast must be your most important meal. It must also include energy-supporting foods.

You will simply have to cut down on the amount of each you eat. It will not be necessary for you to weigh and count everything you eat, but it will be to your advantage to learn more about your calorie intake. The value of your food is measured in calories. You can have a dream of a figure and losing weight can be fun as long as you know you can eat meat and potatoes, jam or jelly, cookies and candy, bread and butter . . . and you can as long as you keep the servings down to a minimum. What's worse? Cutting down or cutting out?

You must learn to refuse second helpings as they go past. Your potatoes will be just as delicious with less gravy. It's fattening. Instead of ice cream and cake, take one or the other. Your sandwiches will be just as tasty with butter or mayonnaise but not both. Cut down on the amount of fried foods included in your daily diet. You'll look and feel better if your fish or meat is broiled or baked. Watch your hand on the amount of sugar you use on cereals and fruits. Try a little vinegar dressing on your salads for a change. Fresh leaves of lettuce and other salad greens lose their nutritional value when they become limp from an overdose of mayonnaise or other rich salad dressings.

GOOD EATING HABITS

Losing weight is just a matter of making good eating habits out of your bad ones. Good food, when eaten properly and moderately, can make a more attractive you. It's not a bad idea to have a calorie chart close by. Check it occasionally. Count the calories for a few days, until you're familiar with the count. When your appetite is reduced to a minimum, you can stop counting. Your eating habits will be normal and the weight will begin to drop. It will be hard, at first. Like all your other accomplishments, losing weight cannot be done in a hurry.

P O U N D   P O O R

Being too skinny and wanting to gain weight is just as worrisome as being too fat and wanting to lose. Fat people are fat because they overeat. Skinny people are the way they are because they don't eat enough. The "whispering campaign" is usually at work on overweight girls, but when your figure looks like an undernourished scarecrow, then you get the "sympathy" treatment. With every glance, it seems that people are feeling sorry for you. You'd rather they didn't look at all. That would suit you just fine. But this makes you feel very uncomfortable. Just like your fat friends, you want to pull yourself away from things . . . and people. You slump and slouch, trying to hide your leanness, which only makes it more noticeable, and your posture bad.

If you fit into this picture, you're impatient. Remember the advice given to the heavy girl . . . it takes time! It will take even longer to gain weight. Your eating habits must change. Even when they do, you may not gain an ounce for the longest time. But making the change will be great for you. Now you'll eat enough to keep a bird alive, when in the past you didn't. You just don't like food. That will change too. If your health is good, you have an excellent chance of putting on a few pounds gradually, as you grow older.

Check your health record. If it's not as good as it should be, this could be a reason why your weight is below normal. A glandular condition could also contrib-

ute to loss of weight. Any internal disturbance is another
reason. Whatever the reasons, someone "in the know"
can tell you, right off the bat, what must be done about it.
After sizing you up, it may be agreed that you are all right
just as you are, for the time being, anyway. Feel assured
that if your health is in good shape and you have the
necessary pep to keep you going, you have nothing to
really worry about. But if you're weak, weary and weight-
less, you need to do something about weight-building.

In a way, you're lucky. It's always better to be under
than over. If you're just a pound or two under your normal weight, cut out some of your activity and eat more.
Your fat friends hate you for it, but you can eat all the
fattening foods that they can't afford to look at. Eating
rich high calorie goodies must be done with moderation,
even by skinny you. Too much is bad for your complexion. If you have the kind of skin that breaks out easily, go
slow and make sure you're eating the foods that produce
smooth facial beauty. Even with a greater intake of more
fats and sweets than those who are overweight, a shortage of vitamins is still another reason for shortage of
pounds. Lots of green vegetables and plenty of fresh fruit
must be combined with the other foods you eat daily.
Although some fruits and vegetables are low in calories,
they are very necessary to your good looks and your
health.

EAT ALL YOU WANT

An increase of food intake is vital to gaining weight.
Whether you like it or not, you must eat. Add to the
number of daily meals with some heavy nutritious snacks
in-between. Your meals must be carefully planned, with
variety from day to day. Food is the most essential re-
quirement for your everyday living, whether or not you
have a weight problem. Your health, your looks and the
function of your body depend on the food you eat each

day. Approach your daily eating habits seriously and intelligently. Eat more of the foods you've learned to like (and even some you say you don't like, but are good body-builders). Eat more of the foods that add pounds. Have more cream on your cereals. Eat more bread with more butter. Have extra helpings of jams and jellies, gravies and cream sauces, extra mayonnaise and salad dressings. All these extras will fill out the lean spots. At first, it will not be easy to adjust your eating habits. It will be gradual, but the change is necessary.

Underweight girls needn't think that overloading their stomach with heavy foods in the mornings will help them gain weight in a hurry. Heavy foods in the morning only give you a slow, lazy, dull start, taking away all your energy and staying with you most of the day.

LIQUIDS HELP

Just for the heck of it, try a moderately planned breakfast, backed up later on with a mid-morning snack of milk, cookies, toast or graham crackers and see how much better you feel . . . and look. Get all the liquids you can into your diet. They are important, too. At your age, you should drink at least three glasses of milk each day. If you're underweight, your quota should be a quart a day. Try a thick malted milk with an egg between meals, and drink an extra glass of milk, warmed, before you go to bed at night. That last glass will put some weight on your body and relax your nerves for a good night's sleep. Include fruit juices (fresh ones are better) and above all several glasses of water.

GOOD LOOKING MEALS

If you help with the meal suggestions and planning, this is when you can use your imagination and good sense about meal planning. This is a fine time to try some of the dishes you've learned to prepare in cooking classes in school. Share your ideas and knowledge. Plan attractive ways to prepare and serve the meals you and your family eat daily, even though they are economy foods you're eating. No matter how low or high priced the food is, it always tastes better when it's prepared in a new way and served attractively. To increase your weight, your meals must be attractive enough to encourage you to eat. Boost your appetite by making your meals look like a supermarket display. Budgets are good. We all must watch our "pennies," but it doesn't pay to skimp on meals when you're trying to gain weight. If you or your family head are watching the budget, you can always find inexpensive, nutritious foods that are not just delicious, but healthy. If it is at all possible, stay away from leftovers. Try to cook enough just for one meal. After spending the night in the refrigerator, foods loose their nutritional value. When you're concerned about your figure, you must have some say about the foods you eat. When you have a finger in the meal-planning, you can be sure that the necessary foods are included in your daily eating plan.

COUNTING CALORIES

The experts say that the average teen-age girl should have around 2,500 calories a day. If you're "average," there's not much for you to worry about. The amount of energy you burn up each day must also be considered. Girls who are overweight generally don't burn up enough energy. The weight slows them down. On the other hand, the underweight girls burn up more energy faster than they can re-store it. This is one of the reasons why it takes longer for the skinny girls to gain weight. The thin girls, in good health, are constantly on the move. Now, if your figure is not average, you know what's ahead for you.

As a rule, your calorie intake decreases with your age. As you get older and you are between sixteen and twenty years old, your calorie intake should drop to around 2,300 to 2,400 each day. If your weight increases with your age, you may not need as many calories. Your weight not only varies with your age but with your body build. If you weigh too much or not enough, work with it, and start to build a body that will be one of beauty and one that you will be proud of.

CHECK BODY MOVEMENTS

Things must be done more slowly when you're trying to gain weight. Instead of rushing and running through the day, ease up on the energy and take more time to get things done. Rest as often as you can. Walking is good, but cut down on that too. Don't do an errand on foot when you can ride. Don't stand when you can sit. The more relaxed you are, the more easily your food will be digested. You'll enjoy your food more, you'll feel better and slowly the pounds will begin to add up. Vitamins, taken daily, are good but only if they are prescribed for you. Take them as directed. They will increase your appetite and help your general health.

Now, if you're one of the thousands that want to lose weight, you will be surprised that there will be no diets listed here for you to follow. You know already that if you're over fifteen pounds, this is too much weight for you to handle the weight-loss by yourself. If you're just a few pounds over, use some of the hints and suggestions provided here and this will be all the dieting you'll need. Be clever. Use your head. Ease up on second helpings. It's better if you can push yourself away from the table with a slight feeling of emptiness. After a few hours, fill up that vacant spot with something light, low in calories, but filling.

EXERCISE CONTROLS POUNDS

Once your weight is under control, keep it that way. It will be easy with exercise. The right diet and just enough exercise will help you mold the figure you've dreamed about. Exercise will keep your body flexible, making it easy to move about. A normal figure needs exercise to keep the body graceful and youthful. The overweight figure needs exercise to tighten and firm loose flabby muscles as the body sheds some of the unwanted pounds. In the reverse, it fills some of the empty spots for the underweight figure. Exercise works up the circulation, making all parts of your body function with greater ease. It puts a look of good health in your face.

MAKE IT FUN

There are many different ways to exercise. It will be fun finding those that are best for you.

CHECK WITH THE DOCTOR

The doctor may suggest exercise for you. If it has been a long time since your last visit, check with him before you begin a steady routine of exercising. This applies even if you think your health is perfect. It's just better this way. The exercise you get going back and forth to school, up and down the stairs, on and off the bus, in and out of the car, is not enough. This is exercise, all right, and tiresome at times. You're using the same muscles over and over again; others aren't being used at all.

There are hundreds of complicated hard-to-do exercises. Some of them come with a guarantee that you'll gain or lose weight . . . all over or in spots. They just may do the things they promise, if anyone stayed with them long enough to find out. It is true, if they are done correctly, day in, day out, month in and month out, you might eventually see a change in the shape of things. Exercising is no one-time-only proposition. You have to stick with it. It's steady, hard work and it takes time before things begin to happen. Don't become discouraged if you don't see quick changes.

DAILY DOSES

Don't expect the exercises you practice daily to do the impossible. You cannot change the position of your bosom, take fat off your arms, fill out your legs, fatten your backsides, by doing a few bends and turns each day. There is more to it than that. Inches and pounds of flesh will not drop to the floor after a bend here and a stretch there. But the same bends and stretches can help you discipline your body and its movements. With more concentration placed on the firmness of your body and its muscles, there will never be a need for special exercises that are hard to continue. Easy to manage pulls, bends and twists can relieve your body of tension brought on by a hard day's work or play. Daily exercises will help you to preserve your body firmness through your teen years and later. As you get older your muscles will get flabby and lazy without attention having been given to them during your early years. Too much stress cannot be placed on body discipline for girls in their teens.

ACTIVE SPORTS

If you're active in sports, your muscles are getting a good workout. Tennis, basketball, swimming, skiing, playing golf (which is taught in many schools), are just a few games that keep you in shape. They are all good for muscle toning and spot reducing. Start with a game of tennis . . . real or imaginary. If you don't have a real game going, go through the motions . . . swing your arms, bend your body, stretch your torso. This imaginary game will keep you prepared and in shape for the real one when it comes along. Take a game of golf . . . on the green or in your living room. It's good exercise anywhere you play it. With the club in your hand and the green all around you, you can't escape the good it will do for your body. But in the living room, you're required to do more work. Make the same swinging and twisting motions. They are just as good for your body inside the house or out.

Play it cool when you're in the pool. Swimming the length of the pool and back again keeps you in shape for the next race. But occasionally, cool it with some neat tricks that make trim figures. Even if you're so good you don't need the side step ladder, use it anyway once in a while. From down below, pull up on the arms, take the second or third steps as you pull. This adds firmness to the chest and bosom muscles . . . tightening up the arm muscles as you pull. Floating on your back is lazy and relaxing. Make your floating pay off. Easy and gently, with a firm twist to the body . . . quickly turn. Repeat several times, twisting and turning the body in both directions.

DANCE ROUTINE

"Jerking," "twisting" and "skating" through some of the latest dance steps is also a good way to stop the sag in over-all body muscles. With the ease and grace of the waltz left back in the dark ages, almost any of the new dance steps provide enough body exercise to last till the next dance session. If you're not active in sports and you don't do any of the "action-packed" dance steps, you've got a problem. Practice by yourself, go through the motions. When the opportunity to do either knocks, you'll show talent you didn't know you had.

STRETCHING AND MUSCLE TONING

Whatever your weight problems may be, you can't afford to be without planned exercises each day. Start the day off with exercises—right in your bed! The moment you open your eyes, after a good night's sleep, stretch before you get out of bed. This is a perfect way to pull in the slack that settled during the night. A good stretch will encourage circulation.

As you lie there, flat on your back, stretch for all you're worth. Imagine someone pulling you, by your feet, right out of bed. Stretch your neck muscles. Roll your head slowly . . . pulling as you roll from side to side. With your arms at your side, stretch both at the same time, hard, pulling right down the side of your body . . . like trying to touch your toes. While in bed, try these exercises, and think up some of your own. See how good they will make you feel and look. When your feet hit the floor, stretch, stretch, again and again! Feel the muscles pulling? You are getting limber. You really feel like going now. With five or ten minutes spent this way each morning, you'll speed through your morning routine feeling alive and doing things will be so much easier. If you do your exercises at the same time, each day, soon your posture is more perfect and the carriage of your body will be so much more graceful. Automatically your shoulders will ease back into place where they belong, your head goes high and your body moves with ease and confidence.

MAKE SITTING PAY OFF

It is said that today's teen-agers sit too much. Think about it . . . before you fight back. You sit on the way to school (if you start early enough to fight for a seat). You sit most of the day in school. You sit to listen to your favorite radio program or to read a book. You sit at a movie or a concert. You sit to watch television. Naturally, you sit to eat your meals. But when you sit do you sit tall, or do you slump and slouch during these sitting periods? If you're taking advantage of these sitting sessions . . . figurewise, that is, great. If you slump and throw your entire body out of line, then you're playing an unfair game with your posture and your digestion. But if you sit tall with all the muscles pulled in where they belong, you're doing wonderful things for your figure. The complainers go on to say, "this is the lazy era . . . everything is made easy for teen-agers." This may be true, but make every moment pay off for you. Even while you're sitting, exercise.

EASY, EASY EXERCISES

The very first thing to do is pull, pull in with all your might on those tummy muscles. Hold in for the count of ten, release and repeat. Keep this up as long as you can, as often as you can during the day, and you'll have the flattest, firmest, front ever. Tightening up and pulling in when you sit will provide a figure that diets couldn't touch. Pull yourself together and you'll be much more relaxed, your posture will be better and your body will be prettier.

As you sit, keep your ankles slim and stir up circulation through your feet and legs by drawing imaginary circles with your feet. With your legs crossed, circle the foot that's in the air. First in one direction and in the other, pulling, as you circle. You can do this on a bus, while you are watching TV, in a movie and lots of other places where you will not disturb other people. You can do your body a lot of good by hanging and pulling on the overhead strap in a bus if you're not lucky enough to get a seat. Don't just stand there, pull and stretch every muscle in your stomach. You can feel that pull from the pit of your stomach, up your arm, and you feel like a new person by the time you reach your destination. All these tightening-up methods can be done all during the day and no one need know your exercise secret. This will help you overcome some of your lazy body habits. Who would have ever thought that just sitting down and standing up could do wonders for your body if done correctly?

EXERCISE WHILE YOU WORK

When household chores face you, don't be so quick to climb up the kitchen ladder when something is needed from one of the top shelves. Stretch for it first. Exercise as you work. Dusting the furniture, scrubbing floors, picking up dropped articles, cleaning high, not-easy-to-reach spots and washing windows need not be faced grimly. Just don't allow weak, weary muscles to run wild and unnoticed. Pull them in . . . tighten them up . . . and keep them in their proper place. This is one of the easiest and quickest ways to keep your body slimmed down and muscles toned up.

One of the world's outstanding beauty experts says "dieters must train their muscles against the return of weight." The more time you spend on "tightening-up" exercises, the quicker you will see results and the longer your figure will remain at its "near perfect" size.

If you're serious about this, you can take your shape one step further. Plan an exercise program, one that you will stick with. A few minutes each day is all you need. If your time is jammed in the morning, try for the afternoon, or better still, at night. Exercising at about the same time, each day, will bring the best results. For most people, the morning is the best time. Try some of the exercises listed here. They are not harmful. They are easy to do and beautiful body-builders. They build body firmness and guarantee elegant, feminine grace.

MOULDING YOUR FIGURE

Before you start, to get full value from your exercise program, get all the clumsy, loose or too-tight clothing out of the way. A leotard or comfortable bathing suit that doesn't cut or bind gives you plenty freedom. If your program is planned for the morning, your birthday suit is as good as any. Or you might try just a pair of panties and your bra, as long as they do not cut or confine the body.

1. Stand tall; feet slightly apart. Find a mark (picture or object) on the wall behind you. Let this be your target. With arms outstretched and feet planted firmly on the floor, twist as far to the right as your body will go. Keep hips straight. Reverse the turn, twist to the left. You may not see your mark, at first, but you will in time. This is a wonderful waist-whittler and at the same time firms the arm and bosom muscles. You will feel the tension on the muscles. Do it five times each way and increase the count, as you improve. If the pull hurts in spots, don't give up. The harder it is for you, the better workout your muscles get.

2. Another good but easy exercise for the waist, is to keep the same position (feet slightly apart). With your hands on your hips, bend as far over to the right as you can go . . . pull and stretch as you bend. Bring body back up to position. Bend to the left. If this one seems too easy, drop your arms to your sides. Let your fingers touch the side of your legs. Go through the same side bending motion . . . first to the right and then to the left. Let your fingers be your guide and with each bend stretch them longer, lower to another spot.

3. For flattening the stomach, put your feet together this time, arms overhead, stretched as high

as you can get them. Slowly bend and stretch as you touch the tip of your toes. Bring the body back up to the starting position and pull as high as you can with your arms. Relax. Again, with stomach muscles pulled in, repeat the bend. Remember the secret is to try these exercises just a few times in the beginning. This one will take a little time before you can increase your count. It will do a much more effective job if you exercise daily and increase your count as you do so. It's much easier than knocking yourself out during the first try and then giving up. It's the continuation of the pulling and stretching that does the work. This is the only way the body defects can be corrected.

4. Since the stomach is usually the most worrisome area, here's another one for it. Lie flat on the floor, body stretched out long and straight. Arms should be at your sides, head lifted a few inches from the floor, legs together, toes pointed. Lift one leg slowly, a short distance from the floor. Try the other leg. Now work this "scissor" motion in rhythm.

5. The make-believe bicycle ride is a good flattener for the tummy. This one pulls the leg muscles and trims inches off flabby hips. Lie on the floor with your legs and hips up as high as you can support them in the palm of your hands. The main support comes from your shoulders and your elbows. Rotate your legs in mid-air . . . like a real bicycle ride. With a little practice, each day, you will soon discover that these simple exercises will not tire you out, but will actually pep you up.

6. Another easy and effective exercise slims the hips. Sit on the floor. Bring your feet together with the soles of feet touching . . . knees stretched and bent. With palms of hands resting on knees, rock and roll from side to side. Keep your back straight and shoulders up in position. This one is fun-filled

and a thorough muscle-pulling job is done on the back of the body as well as the front muscles.

7. Here is another tummy tightener, one that you can really count on. Your body is stretched straight on the floor, your arms at your sides. Lift your head slightly from floor. Lift your feet about the same distance. Raise the legs, together, to a straight, overhead position. Lower them slowly and more slowly as they near the floor. If you can't feel that pull in your stomach . . . stick with it . . . you will. This one comes with a guarantee that makes every muscle know they must work . . . for you!

EXERCISE YOUR WAY THROUGH A BATH

Another good time for exercising is bath time. While you're sitting and soaking, bend over and try to touch your toes. After a few tries, sit back and raise the legs, alternately, with rhythm. This is not too easy, but once you've mastered it, it will do the trick.

I think you can see that with every simple, easy-to-do exercise, your body will get a good tugging and pulling . . . just what it needs. Design some exercises of your own to fit your own individual needs, but nothing outlandish and impossible.

If you can exercise to music, a record, the radio or to your own tune, this working period will be so much more enjoyable. It may be even more fun to exercise with a friend, or with a group. Check the program of your neighborhood Y.W.C.A. Work out with a group there, or with one at a nearby school or community center. Most programs have included "figure control" for young figures. Don't let them go to waste.

5

This Is Your Hair

There was a time when the black female thought she was all alone with hair problems. But because a large percentage of black and other non-white females have hair that is excessively curly or kinky, they have had to resort to hot straightening combs and curling irons to come out with hair that was fairly presentable. For years, this was a secret that many women hid behind locked doors. Today, the secret is out and hair straightening is in and there's nothing to be ashamed of. Everybody's doing it! Even white females, dissatisfied with their natural curl, use straightening combs and other straighting methods. Some have even "ironed" out the curl right on the ironing board. As quiet as it's kept, the chemical straightners were originally formulated for whites, with kinky hair (or extremely curly, if you will). Your hair and your hair problems, was not considered at all, so you have no reason to be embarrasssed when the subject is discussed.

Hair styles among non-white females today are just as smooth, lustrous and attractively styled as those of any other race. Most hair products companies, who at one time were only interested in keeping the already straight hair in perfect shape, became aware of the hair problems of those females with uncontrollable curly hair and decided to do something about it. Was there any wonder? When you know that we spend thousands of dollars each year on hair care products, you can easily understand why.

The successful black-owned hair products companies, already knowing the problems from the roots out, have refined some of the old stand-bys and formulated new products that keep the hard-to-manage hair beautiful and lovely. Every effort and lots more money than you can count has been spent to keep each strand of black hair something the individual can be proud of. Some of the new hair products have cut down or even cut out constant trips to the hairdresser.

STRAIGHT HAIR

If it's straight hair you want, you can have it with very little trouble and time. Smooth sweet-smelling cremes, known as hair relaxers, have become just as popular as straightening combs. Once applied, as directed, they are known to relieve the hair of its natural curl. Even spray straighteners have proved successful for some. For excessively tightly-curled and kinky hair, cremes and sprays were not powerful enough to straighten the hair so the wearer could get managable "dead straight" hair styles. Many of these heads turned to permanent straighteners. The popularity (and short-termed success) of these powerfully-strong straighteners caused many a girl to turn in relief from every-two-week trips to the beauty parlor for a hard hot comb pressing job. For those heads that could stand it, the permanents worked successfully. A quick shampoo and a wet set was the answer to any one of the new hair styles popular with the swinging young teen group.

The permanent, however, is only permanent until new hair grows in to replace the process-treated hair. Hitting the black communities like the A-bomb, some of the early straightening methods proved fatal for hundreds of women with a strong desire for lively, smooth, silky-straight hair. All such products are not do-it-yourself items and must be used only by professional hairdressers, and even then it's at your own risk. There are still a large percentage of creme straighteners, even though they are loaded with powerful chemicals, that do not successfully straighten hard-textured hair. The failure of hair straighteners only make the straightening comb more important and valuable. Today it is just as popular as it ever was.

The hot comb may be a nuisance, but for many it's the only answer to straight hair styles. A large number of hairdressers, much experienced with caring for tightly-curled hair, rely heavily on the hot comb and wouldn't change it for all the chemical products in the world. If you are a do-it-yourselfer, check the heat of your hot comb and curling iron. Overheated combs destroy the internal structure of the hair and you end up with burned-off ends or hair with an over-straightened look.

If you find yourself on this side of the fence, and you've been just sitting there wishing for the "fairy godmother" to come down and touch you with her magic wand that will give you a new head of hair, you can put that out of your mind. Put your time to better use. To date the fairy godmother, if there is such a thing, just hasn't been that generous. Sitting there wishing and wanting the impossible won't work. If you want a head of hair that you will be proud of and happy with, you have to work for it. Nothing comes easily. You work day and night. It is a never-ending job if you want a clean, easy-to-manage head of hair.

MAKE IT NATURAL

In recent years, a large group of young black girls decided to forget the whole thing. They gave up the straightening comb and all the other gadgets and products for hair straightening results. Going "natural" was the "in" look for them. This "natural" look started tongues wagging. They talked and gossiped from the Golden Gate bridge in California to the one in Brooklyn, New York! Making this big jump from straight to kinky, these kids quietly shook up the entire nation. There was much talk about "do you or don't you like it." Those girls and even boys, deciding on this look for themselves, couldn't have cared less. Those who did not identify their hair-dos as the "natural look," preferred to call their bushy hair the "Afro" or "African look" instead. Either way, the look is the same. It has been expressed in a loud clear voice that individuals choosing this new hair style have become amazingly aware of their African heritage. It further proved to others, just in case they had forgotten, that the black female does exist. "And don't you forget it!" sounded thousands of young voices all over the nation. If you wish to create new standards and prove racial pride for yourself, this might be your answer to a hair styling problem. In this present generation you can cater to your vanity anyway you chose. Even if your "natural" glory requires more than a "wash and a shake," you might find such a hair style more attractive to your facial beauty and easier to care for.

REGULAR CARE

If your mind tells you to move from one extreme to another, you can't escape giving your hair daily attention and proper cleaning care. The "natural" looks like a time-saver, and no doubt it is. But even with less hair on your head, it still must be clean.

Some girls have ended up with the "Afro" look whether they liked it or not. This was simply due to improper care, a serious illness or over-powerful chemicals that broke the hair right down to the roots. An unhealthy scalp is always the basic reason for unhealthy hair. Just like your face, your hair gives away all your health secrets. Traces of poor health go right to the top of your head. It will tell of your loss of sleep, worry, tension, your edgy nerves, overwork and strain, acne, that time-of-the-month or any common illness. When your hair just won't work right, won't look right, no matter what you do with it, any one of the above conditions could be the reason for its unsightly appearance.

If you're under the care of the doctor and you're taking prescribed vitamins or tonics, in rare cases some of these medicines may affect the appearance of your hair. Any unusual scalp condition, like sores or pimples or an excessive amount of falling hair, could very well be a warning signal telling you about some inside disturbance. Internal ailments can cause your hair to become dry, dull, lifeless and unmanagable.

Things have never been so good for black hair . . . long or short. No hair problem is so great that it cannot be corrected or greatly improved. Your hair has a right to its own personal beauty, even though it may be pressed hard and straight. There are great numbers of hair products on the beauty shelf in the stores that have been formulated especially for pressed hair. Many of these have been manufactured by experts with long years of experience in this field. To use some of these products effectively, one does not always need professional skill. She needs just the desire and determination to want healthy hair with shining loveliness. That is the dream of every girl . . . regardless of the color of her skin or her choice of hair style.

START WITH A CLEAN HEAD

All experts in the beauty field say that any hair style starts with clean hair. If you know this, and believe it, then it's your job to clean your hair, or have it cleaned. Frequent shampoos are necessary for a healthy scalp. The normal scalp requires washing every ten to fourteen days. If you let it go longer, it is unhealthy and unclean. There is no set rule that tells you how often your hair should be washed. If you have the kind of hair that can be washed every time you're under the shower, lucky for you. But don't let it go any longer than the fourteen day period. Where you live and how you live may depend on how many times you wash your hair in a month. Where you work and where you go to school and what you do, and the quality and texture of your hair will also help in the decision of how many times you wash it. It has been said that too many shampoos will change the condition of the scalp. Shampoos will not harm the scalp any more than frequent washings will harm your face.

The skin that covers your skull is a continuation of the skin that covers your face. It must be cared for in the same way. If you have very dry skin, chances are you will have a dry scalp. If your scalp condition is oily, it works in the same way.

SELECTING SHAMPOOS

If you do your own shampooing or if you have it done, make sure you and your beautician are careful about the shampoo used. Use good judgement and select one that goes deep below the surface of the scalp. Then you know your hair is clean . . . really clean. Every trace of soap must be rinsed away after each application, when you do your own shampooing.

You can do a hairdo job quite successfully at home.

Many girls, just like you, have learned to create groovy hair styles at home. Practice makes it easy, even if you have your hair "done" every two weeks or oftener. In case of emergency, you should be able to do your own hair. Being away at school, traveling or shut-in with a long illness could be just one of the many reasons why you must have some do-it-yourself ability. You should be able to change your hairdo at the drop of a hat. Keep some hair-style tricks up your sleeve, ready in time of need. Doing your own hair can be a snap. An at-home arrangement can be loads of fun, and especially when you arrange a "shampoo session" with a girl friend or neighbor. It will save you money. If your hair requires more than a quick shampoo and rinse for a well-groomed attractive appearance, the at-home arrangement may not work for you. If you know that the best hair care program for you is a regular every two weeks visit to the beauty shop, don't let anything upset this routine. But this arrangement cuts a big hole right in the middle of the budget. So cut down on the amount of money you spend on candy, sodas and the like and spend it on hair care needs instead.

BEAUTICIANS WORK FOR YOU

Selecting the right beautician is just as important as selecting the right doctor. Make sure yours has a good reputation and does a professionally-right job for you. You must ask her questions, too. Ask her about the products she uses on your hair. She will not be too keen on telling too many of her professional secrets, but if she's good and takes a special interest in your hair, she will share some of this information with you. She may go even further, and tell you just why she has selected some of the products for your hair. If you have confidence in her ability, and she understands your hair, you will leave with a head of beauty, once her job is done.

The "natural" or "Afro" looks easy to care for. But even

this short, cropped hair requires regular shampoos, conditioners and frequent trims and shapings. Short, blunt haircuts look best when they are clean with a natural softness and gentle brightness. Many of these "natural" heads still make their regular trips to the beauty shop. Whatever hair style you select for yourself, use the hair products that give it the best look.

PICKING HAIR CARE PRODUCTS

There is a wide selection of shampoos on the market, teamed up with creme rinses to remove snarls. Conditioners smooth the hair to unusual softness and often encourage growth. Almost any conditioner is a real beauty treatment for the hair. Don't forget setting jells and a long list of other products that make hair care easier. Your beautician has an array of products to select from when you place your hair care problems in her hands. Either way, a good shampoo is always the beginning of a beautiful head of hair. A series of thorough rinsings follow the necessary soapings. Hair is dried properly so that ends remain in place . . . unbroken. During the drying process, the scalp muscles should get good exercise. They become weak and sluggish and the growth of the hair is upset if these muscles are not stimulated and active. If your hair is not done at home, your beautician will suggest ways you can give it personal attention between your regular visits to the beauty parlor. The beautician cannot do it all. The work you do at home is just as important as the job she does in the beauty parlor.

FINGER MASSAGING

Daily massaging of the scalp is a must for healthy hair. Start with thumbs placed at the temples (in front of the ears); other fingers are at the hair line. Start to move the fingers into the hair, with a circular motion from the front of the head as far back as you can go. Reverse and start from the back of the head and come forward to the hair line. This exercise will start the blood to flow, loosen dirt and might even encourage the hair to grow. If the scalp is dry and flaky, a touch of lightweight oil or creme at the tip of each finger worked into the scalp as you massage will keep the scalp smooth, adding a natural glow to the hair. A dry flaky scalp can be temporary (nerves, illness, too much hot sun or too much indoor heat). The daily working over your scalp is one of the best scalp-stimulants there is.

ADD A NATURAL SHINE

Cut out loading the scalp with heavy grease. This is a bad habit that should be stopped, immediately. Plastering your hair down with heavy grease catches all the dirt and dust that lights on your head. Try instead one of the greaseless products that lubricate the scalp, but leaves no greasy after-effects. They are formulated to penetrate deep into the scalp, leaving the surface soft and lustrous without a greasy look.

BRUSHING FOR HAIR BEAUTY

Daily brushing is another guaranteed method of putting a healthy shine in your hair. There is much to be said about those one hundred strokes you've heard so much about. Brushing not only removes the dirt and dust, but with the right twist of the wrist an attractive hair style can be brushed right into place. Short hair styles are much more attractive when they are brushed several times a day. Just any brush won't do! The ones with natural bristles do the best job. Brushes with nylon or synthetic bristles are cheaper, but have been guilty of breaking and cutting the hair. The natural bristle brushes cost more but are well worth it. A good brush is a good investment.

Once you've made the investment, it would be a crime to abuse a brush that is doing so many wonderful things for your hair. Keep it clean! You wouldn't think of putting a dirty tooth brush in your mouth, would you? Treat your hair brush with the same respect. A brush with good natural bristles can take many more washings. Wash it every night before going to bed. Add a drop or two of ammonia in hot soapy water, and it will be even cleaner.

SWEATING SCALPS

Another serious condition is a sweating scalp. If this is true with you, more trips to the beauty parlor are in order. But, if you're clever, shampoo it yourself between your two-week visits. Your hair style may not be great, but your scalp will be clean-smelling and healthy. Perspiration in your head may only be slight, but if neglected, as on your body, it encourages an unpleasant odor. Heavy-handed use of hair oil is another offender. It the perspiration is more frequent than you can deal with, and makes the hair "go back" at the roots and around the edges, the purchasing of your own pressing comb, for a light touch-up job, may be another good investment. If the shampoo is older than fourteen days, the heat touching dirty hair will break it as soon as the contact is made. Remember to be extra careful!

For years now, scientists in this field have been experimenting with products that promise to keep the hair "straight." If you decide on one of the many "straighteners," and you are certain your hair can take the dynamic power they possess . . . buy the best on the market. Your hair is your crowning glory. Wear it any way you like. It's yours! But always be cautious about the preparations you use on your hair. Know all there is to know about those that interest you. Don't be fooled by high powered advertisements. The products that work successfully for others may leave you without hair.

Oils and cremes and curl relaxers are popular hair aids. They protect the roots from moisture and dampness. They too require careful consideration. Any product that says it will perform unusual duties must be carefully checked and cleared before using with your beautician or a professional in this field. Stay clear of new unheard of products. Use only those products that have been accepted and approved. When you know everything there is to know about your hair, only then can you be thinking about a hair style.

DO-IT-YOURSELF

If you are a do-it-yourselfer, changing your hair style can be a snap. You should be able to do at least three styles. If you go to the beauty shop, after that creation begins to flop and fade, you should be able to step in and take it from there. With little practice, you should be able to put it back into place or create a new one. There's nothing better to pull you right out of a rut and give you a new lease on life than a new hair style. Doing things with your own hair can be an asset, not to mention the money it will save you. Running to the beauty shop for a "hair comb" puts a big hole right in the middle of the budget, and is unnecessary. If you take enough interest in your appearance, you will want to do some of these things for yourself.

If you depend on your hairdresser to keep you in "top notch" condition, let's hope she is up on what's new on the market. If she is, she will not turn you out with deep-set artificial waves and tight curls that just don't form new natural-looking hair styles. The coarsest textured hair requires a minimum of heat. Even with the straightening comb and hot curling irons, this hair can be finished with silky smoothness. Tight-set curls are old-fashioned and unattractive when you want them to be the basis for a fashionable hair style. Your hair style should be one that is simple, neat and uncomplicated. Be able to manage it yourself. Above all, it must be one that is best suited for you, your personality, and your life. Fancy complicated hairdos can make you look foolish and out of place. While the beautician is at work, help in the decision making. She will be more pleased with her work when she knows that her job has been one that pleases you. Remember that the appearance of your hair makes a definite change in your over-all appearance.

CURLERS, ROLLERS AND BOBBY PINS

Today, most hair styles are set with rollers. Even hair that one time thought it couldn't exist without hot curling irons. All textures of hair look ten times better styled when set with rollers. Over-heated curling irons and straightening combs can be dangerous to the hair. Too much heat destroys the internal structure of each strand, making it difficult to hold up under any hair style. Forget hot irons when you use creme or lotion straighteners. The two just don't go to-gether!

If your decision turns to heat, even loose curls set with a curling iron need some help to stay in place. At-home setting with rollers, dry or wet, gives the hair body and adds finished beauty to any style. Curling irons come in all sizes . . . from regular to king size. The king size is sometimes known as the "bop" iron. It gives a great look to short hair. The short ends are just bopped under, not making a real curl, but turning wild, blunt ends into position. All this forms orderly smoothness.

When you stock up on rollers, depending on your hair

style or its length, you might need several sizes . . . the large ones for the top and smaller ones to catch short back ends. It is dangerous to sleep in rollers—dangerous to your health and comfort. Tight rollers, clips and bobby pins have been known to split ends and break the hair. Without rollers, at night, the hair will stay in place with a little brushing and pampering at bedtime. Cover and tie up the hair in safe keeping, putting every strand in place, and the next morning it will still be beautiful and attractive. It is interesting to note that there are now rollers, which heated before use, will add instant curl, and in a jiffy you're ready to go. Keep up with what's new. Invest your money wisely. Buy only those products that work effectively for you.

A HAIR STYLE FOR YOU

All this may sound easy, but it isn't . . . if you haven't decided on a hair style for yourself. Making this decision can be done at the snap of your finger, if you know your face and its shape. The rule still holds firm that the shape of the face must have certain hair styles to look more attractive. If you're not too sure about the shape of your face, tie a kerchief around your head, hiding every strand of hair. Take a good look. While you're looking at the outer edge, check closely the facial features. They figure into this important decision. Hair styles can add width to the nose and mouth. This is important! Every decision you make for yourself must be one that will make you a more attractive person. What about that face of yours?

Is yours fat and round, long and oblong, boxy and square or is it shaped like a triangle? Look closely and determine which you possess. Once you've made up your mind, it will be easy to go on. Shy away from hair styles that exaggerate the shape of your face. If your face displays a definite roundness, you will not want to emphasize that facial fullness. You want a hair style that will give the illusion of a longer line. If you can achieve this, you've done a great job.

ROUND FACE

Arrange your hair in several styles and see the difference each will make to the shape of your face, as you stand before your mirror. A center or side part can make a great difference; it can change the shape of your face completely. The most difficult shape to work with is the fat, round face. Short hair that ends just below your ears and cuts into your face at the widest point, makes that point seem wider. If your hair is short, but combed back and up in the front, the face immediately takes on a longer look. No matter how important flat straight bangs are to the fashion scene, they are no good for the round face. But a soft naturally curled bang that extends out or over to one side will add length and height to your face. Poufs and fluffs are to be avoided.

LONG OR OVAL FACE

Hair piled high on your head will only make a long rectangular or oval face look longer. You can widen that long face with side fullness. Easy, casual forehead treatment, to one side, helps to break the long line.

TRIANGULAR SHAPED FACE

A face that presents a high square forehead and narrows sharply toward the chin is known as triangular. How simple it is to cut down on the width of the forehead with a softness that moves down into the face . . . adding fullness into the area that is narrow and pointed. The right hair comb can actually change the shape of your head. If it flattens out or points up in the wrong place, a gentle lifting, teasing or puffing of hair in that particular spot will delete any ugly features so even you will forget they ever existed.

Being a copy-cat is bad anyway you look at it. Copying hair styles can be downright disastrous. If an exact hair style you see in a book or magazine or on a friend can be applied to you and your face, and you think you just can't live without it, by all means try it. Just remember, if it's a short close cut, you're stuck with it until it grows out. Discovering and working out your own hair styles is so much more fun. When you have settled on a style for yourself, remember it is supposed to do interesting things for your face. You can change your hair style as quickly as you can change your mind . . . just make a change that you, yourself, can handle.

KNOW WHAT IS BEST FOR YOU

The way you arrange your hair can emphasize your interesting facial features and deemphasize those that are unattractive and uninteresting. Select a style that is easy for you to manage . . . one that doesn't require constant "fixing." Bypass the styles that depend on a thousand hair pins or bobby pins to keep curls and waves in place. It's bothersome to have hair equipment falling out of place every time your head turns. Know your limitations and stay within them. Keep your styles young.

Every face and personality type cannot and should not wear the Afro . . . no matter what you're trying to prove. If your facial characteristics are good and this style forms a perfect frame for your face . . . go to it! With all these good features going for you, even with this dramatic change you're a picture of beauty. If your hair doesn't have the "stiffness" to stay up in place, even with good shaping, tight pin curls could be your answer. Combed through, brushed out and mildly teased, it will give you the same look. A little hair spray will give added insurance and beauty.

Heavy-duty hair spray on outlandish hair styles, glued in place, has gone forever . . . we hope! Natural hair beauty is what every girl is searching for today. It's up to you to find yours with the just right style for your face.

CURLING AND STYLING

If you've given pin curls a chance and you had no luck, your hair either had too much oil on it or it was dirty. When your hair is greasy and dirty not even the heat from the curling iron will leave a curl. The grease weighs your hair down and the dirt doesn't give the curl a chance to set. If your hair is clean and has a minimum amount of oil, your hair will curl softly and naturally with almost no help at all. Pin curl it dry. When curls are all in place, spray generously with one of the hair sprays that have been formulated especially for pressed hair. If your hair doesn't require heat, any good reliable hair spray will do. The spray encourages the curls to stay put once they are clipped or pinned. They also protect them after combing from changing their position when exposed to the wind and dampness. There will be no straying ends or drooping curls. The newly improved sprays will not leave your hair hard and dry and there will be no flaky crust when you comb through your hair.

The secret to pin curling is always to be positive with your curls. If you want them to go in one direction, when combed out, the curl must be set in that direction. For instance if you want the curl going back and away from your face, wrap the hair around your finger going in that direction. If it's the other way, just change the direction of the curl. For perfect results all ends must be neatly tucked in place before the curl is pinned or clipped. Your hair will be more healthy with pin curls instead of over-heated hot-iron curls.

HAIR CUTTING

No matter how good you are with at-home tricks, hair cutting is one job that should be left for professional hands. Improper use of the scissors or clippers can be dangerous to the hair and its growth. Carrying your hair-cutting ability too far can spoil your looks forever. It's nice when you can have things done for you. You feel so good when you know they are done right. So an occasional haircut may be all you need to give you that "new look" feeling.

Avoid hair dressing fads. Fancy dyes, streaks and sun tips should be put aside for a later date. If you use all the tricks in the book now, there will be no new thrills for you when you get older. Keep your appearance young just as long as you can. You may have to dig deep for some of these ideas, in your later years, to fulfill that desire for youth. Don't push yourself too fast. There's plenty of time for grown-up tricks, when you're grown up.

GLAMOROUS AND GLITTERING

Think twice before you allow yourself to be all lit up with glamorous glittering hair gadgets that are elaborate and fancy. Choose instead those that are simple and youthful in design. Hair ornaments that are more useful than decorative such as plain tortoise-shell, gold or silver barettes, combs and bobby pins should fill your every need. For dress-occasions stick to the hair ornaments that are not too overdone. Rhinestone clips, rhinestone or pearl (or both) tiaras, head bands, ribbon bows and small flower clips and bobby pins are enough to dress up the most elegant gown for girls your age.

CLEAN TOOLS

The number one rule for everything you do is cleanliness. This applies to your hair and its tools. A clean head of hair must be tended and cared for with clean grooming tools. Never use dirty combs and brushes. They must be washed every time you wash your hair, and so much the better if you can manage a clean-up job in between shampoos. A clean comb and brush will keep your hair clean longer. Clean tools make it possible to remove dirt and dust easily. This includes bobby pins, small hair combs, curlers, hair nets and hair ribbons. Someone has suggested that to keep these small pieces from getting lost in the wash, drop them into a glass jar (fruit or mayonnaise) of hot soap suds. Cap it securely and shake vigorously. Open the jar and hold it under running water to float and rinse the suds away. Dump the pins and curlers onto a towel. Your hair nets and head bands can be washed the same way. Isn't that easy?

The suggestion goes on that those "glitter gadgets" that brighten up your hair styles now and then can be kept glittering by using an old toothbrush to remove dirt and to keep the stones polished and bright. Ribbons can be kept fresh and crisp by swishing them through warm suds and rinses in this same "jar washing" method. Ironing sometimes can ruin them. To avoid this, wrap them while they are still damp around the bathroom or kitchen hot water pipe if it is exposed. They'll dry in a jiffy and there won't be a wrinkle in sight. They can be tucked away into your ribbon box . . . ready for use when you need them.

ADD A HAIR PIECE

The popularity of wigs, hairpieces, falls and attachments makes it impossible to end this chapter and not mention their use for girls your age.

If you're faced with disaster, and you could just die before showing your head (it has happened many times), I can't think of anything nicer than a youthfully styled, head-hugging, all over wig. These are the greatest to cover newly sprouting hair. The waiting-period will be long, depending on the damage. You'll feel that growth of hair will come back much faster, when it's topped with something as "sharp" as this. Using a wig at a time like this gets my big fat "A-O.K." But if you're thinking of investing in a wig just to cut down on hair cleanliness or to cover up hair that has been neglected, you're cheating. You're also adding damage to your natural, young beauty.

On the other hand, if you feel that you just must have one of the inexpensive wigs or hair pieces, purchased in the dime or discount store tuck them away in a decorative box until a real glamour occasion comes along to use them. Don't ever think that a wig makes the routine of hair care easier. They must be cleaned and cared for just like your own hair. It's not as easy as it looks. Even the cheap pieces require steady care and attention if you want an attractive attachment that you will wear with pride and beauty.

6

This Is Your Face

It seems as if with every turn, there's your face; always on the scene. Yes, ninety-nine times out of a hundred, your face is the first part of you to be noticed. It makes the first impression of you. Most often, that impression is the one that sticks.

Never before has your face been so important. Faces like yours are seen everywhere. They pop up in daily newspapers, all over the country, sometimes on the covers of national magazines and inside on news articles, and many times on the fashion pages. It is no longer unusual to see an attractive brown face appear on your television screen. There are girls, looking very much like you, in television commercials and in your favorite TV serials. It's such a good feeling to see these faces in parts you can now be proud of. It is almost a natural to see a brown face representing her race in top notch professional positions. It is not at all unusual to see a face that you can identify with working in areas of medicine, law, science, engineering, world-wide sports events, automation, art and fashion promotion and design. Throughout the business world, there are hundreds . . . you name it and you'll find her there.

SHOW IT WITH PRIDE

Your face is important! You're barking up the wrong tree if you think for one minute that all the faces of these successful women are natural born beauties. They are not. It would be foolish, however, to think that facial beauty did not help. But you know very well that "it takes more than good looks" to succeed in the world. Beauty, so they say, is only skin deep. But real beauty comes deeper than that. A face that is interesting can be much more exciting and attractive than one that is beautiful with nothing to back it up. A face that expresses beauty is far more important. You had nothing to do with the kind of face that has been given to you. You can't turn it in for one you like better. You're stuck with it. It's your job to do the best you can with it. If you think beautifully, act beautifully, walk and talk beautifully, there is no doubt that your face will reflect that beauty . . . a face that will do wonderful things for you. Facial beauty is work, but it succeeds.

You are not alone if you're not completely satisfied with your face as it is. It would be almost impossible to find a girl that is absolutely thrilled with her face, as she sees it. What a satisfying feeling to know that with the aid of cosmetics and your own fingertip magic, you can produce a near-perfect face, one that will please you.

For years, cosmetic companies with the exception of popular black-owned firms, couldn't have cared less about you and your beauty needs. The importance of you and your face has encouraged some changes in the cosmetic industry. It has been clearly understood that a woman would spend her last cent on her face. Anything goes if it will make her face look better. With all the dollars being spent on cosmetics and other facial needs, everybody's jumping on the beauty band wagon. Today most of your beauty needs have, at least, been considered.

IT NEEDS SOME WORK

Now, if your face needs little or no repair, you're one of the fortunate few. But most females have some work to do day after day, trying to make their faces what they want them to be. Some are still dissatisfied. No matter how ordinary or plain you think your face is, it can be one of beauty with the right know-how. The personal care list is long, it is true, and other parts of your body need your attention, but your face deserves an extra measure of consideration.

A lovely face with velvet-smooth skin is as easy as following five simple rules. The first and most important is cleanliness. Eating the right foods and daily elimination make rule two and three. The fourth and fifth stress rest, plenty of fresh air and lots of exercise.

COSMETICS AND FOOD SKIN WORRIES

If your skin is normal, it can take any kind of food without too much difficulty, if you don't overdo it. But you just can't eat everything in sight and expect to have soft, pimple-free skin. The near-perfect skin type makes sure that fresh fruits and vegetables and a good supply of milk and several glasses of water are included in the diet each day. Oil-producing skin should stay away from oily foods. Greasy nuts, fried meats and fish add to the oil supply, making more pimples and bumps.

ALLERGIES

If you are allergic to certain foods and chemicals found in beauty products, particular attention must be given to your choice of foods. Chocolate sodas and candy, shell fish, peanuts, greasy and rich foods create skin care problems for some teen-agers. Others can fly through life eating any foods of their choice with no skin worries at all. If you're one of the lucky ones, your skin will be easy to care for. If you're not, the cosmetic market has supplied you with an arm load of non-allergic products, aiding you to unblemished skin. Be satisfied with the color of your face. Avoid using harsh bleaches that say they will lighten your skin. There hasn't been a cream on the market yet to turn dark skin white. Harsh bleaches do damage to young tender skin. Bleaching creams, used once in awhile, will not do a bleaching job, but they will help remove dried-out, damaged skin. They have been known to remove dark spots and other skin discoloration. A minimum amount of such cream can add a new freshness to dingy, splotchy skin, smoothing the way to a fresh radiant one-color complexion.

FIND YOUR SKIN TYPE

Skin comes in four types . . . normal, dry, oily or a combination of the last two. Place yours in one of these groups before you start your daily care treatment. Regardless of your skin type, your facial beauty must be built on a clean background. Generally, young skins are firm and smooth, and are moisture soaked with natural oil. If this sounds like yours, soap and water washings, once or twice a day, could be all you need. If you are not so blessed, and yours is rough and dry looking, cream cleaning morning and night, combined with the washing, in time will smooth away the dull dry look. For extra special attention, try some of the cleaning foams and jellied soaps that come in jars and tubes. It will be to your advantage to keep up with new skin-care preparations, whether your skin requires special attention or not. Make a habit of visiting cosmetic counters. Familiarize yourself with the products formulated for young skins. You will find a remedy for every skin problem. Even if your budget will allow you to make purchases, don't buy everything you see. You will end up with a medicine chest filled with mistakes if you are not a very careful shopper.

WASHING YOUR FACE IS AN ART

Believe it or not, the art of keeping your face clean can be done with soap and water. Don't believe everything you hear about the harm soap and water can do to facial beauty. These rules do not apply to young healthy-smooth skin, unless it is terribly sick and damaged. Nothing could be nicer for your skin than a soap and water bath.

Splashing the water here and there is all wrong, if you expect to get your face clean. Your hands must always be thoroughly cleaned before they touch your face . . . yes, even before you wash it. Once that is done, work up a good lather with a good toilet soap (if there are no skin problems) on your washcloth or a soft complexion brush. Lather your face all over. Pay particular attention to the nose, chin and forehead. These are the areas that are usually oversupplied with oil. Include your ears and your hair line, always remembering that your neck is a part of your facial clean-up job. Work the soap well into the skin with gentle finger-tip pressure. The soothing touch of your own fingers will stimulate the circulation which helps to remove some of the waste material. The softness of the bristles of a complexion brush is an excellent stimulator—a good habit to form if you haven't done so.

Slow sluggish circulation is one of the main reasons for lumps and bumps that collect under the surface of your skin. After your face has been treated to a good over-all soap massage, it will take several rinsings to remove all signs of soap. Start with warm to hot water, cool the temperature of the water each time and finally make the last dash with cold water. The type of your skin may require you to wash your face more than three times a day, but no matter how high the count, the job must be a thorough one each time.

Skin bumps and pimple problems start with skin that has not had proper cleaning. Some of these bumps and pimples can be washed away with soap and water. If simple problems appear now and are neglected as usual, they grow into serious ones later. Your pores must breathe properly to produce a complexion that is smooth and healthy. They can't breathe at all if they are clogged with oil and dirt.

OILY SKIN

You won't have any trouble seeing the oil on your skin, if it is in abundance. Don't look the second time. You have oily skin. This skin condition is not as bad as one might think. An oily-smooth skin is pretty when soap and water is used to remove some of the oil supply. It's easier removing over-productive oil that comes to the surface of the skin than it is to add moisture to dry skin. When you wash your face, the more soap and water you use each day the better. Select a soap with an oil-free base. If too much oil is left on the face to catch the dirt and dust flying in the air, before long the pores are plugged, and soon after that your face is covered with ugly bumps.

DRY SKIN

For dry, scaly skin the treatment is reversed. Remove the day's dirt with a pure, mild cleansing cream. After two or maybe three clean-up jobs, leave a thin coating of oil on the top surface. With a soap that contains an oil or lanolin base, wash your face. Blot dry, leaving some of the oil in place. As you glide your fingertips over your face, the feeling will be clean and soft.

COMBINATION SKIN

A combination skin is not hard to work with; it just may take a little more time. Each area must be treated individually. Take the oily areas of nose, chin and forehead first. Massage each area with your wash cloth, dampened and rubbed over a cake of soap. Work well into these three parts before you work with the dry area of the cheeks and neck. That area requires lubrication with a mild cream, oil or lotion.

Your skin type has no relation to its color. At one time, it was believed that the texture of darker skins was rough and harsh. This is not true. Look around you and count the number of dark faces that display skins smooth as velvet. Yet on the other hand the count of light or white complexions with blemished, unattractive, rough skin may be high. The color of your skin isn't important anyway. There is no medicine that will change it, so you might as well be satisfied. Keeping your skin clean is important no matter what color it is.

BLACKHEADS AND PIMPLES

If for some reason your face has produced bumps and pimples, this can cramp your style. Blackheads and pimples can mar your facial loveliness and cause you to become self-conscious. You think all eyes are on you and all tongues are wagging, behind your back, about those awful bumps on your face. If you've allowed this to happen, the cream and steam method is one easy way to help you eliminate a simple pimply condition. After a thorough cleaning job to remove all traces of dirt, apply cold cream or any mild lubricant to your face and neck, paying special attention to the affected area. This will help loosen up the clogged pores. Slip into the bathtub and relax in warm, not hot, water. As you ease all the worries from your mind, the steam mixes with the cream, and the dirt that has been hidden in the pores eases up to the surface of your skin. Wring out a clean washcloth in hot water. With it opened up, press it against your face, with extra pressure on the affected parts. Cool the temperature, wring out the cloth again, and repeat until the water is cold. You can finish up with the cold water or a splash of cooling skin lotion. This last step will close the pores again that have been opened by the steam and hot water. After your face has been patted dry your skin will be left lively-clean, smooth and on its way to being clear.

ACNE BUMPS SAY YOU'RE GROWING UP

If pimples get more serious, then a more serious treatment is necessary. Changes in your skin begin to show up during your teen years . . . the adolescence period. At this time, pimples are sure to make an appearance, in one form or another. These adolescence bumps are more commonly called acne. For years, this has been the number one teen-age skin problem. Even boys have acne bumps. This doesn't mean, however, that all teen-agers will have acne. You may be one of the lucky girls who will not be troubled with it at all. If you are less fortunate and big puffy bumps begin to show up on your face, don't be too unhappy and disgruntled. There is a cure for acne. True, acne causes much frustration. These bumps always pop out at the wrong time. Just when you have dreamed of making a good impression and want to put your best face forward . . . something goes wrong. Overnight, it seems, your face breaks out with big ugly bumps. You'll listen, next time, when you hear over and over again, that you must keep your face clean. However, poor face care is not the primary cause of acne, but it can aggravate it. An acne condition means that something has gone wrong with the oil glands. Young skins, with an excessive amount of oil, more than likely will have to deal with acne bumps. Some cases of acne are simple and others are severe. The severe cases are brought on by neglect. Acne bumps will remain on your face for as long as you neglect your skin.

Acne is something you can't fool around with. If mistreated and neglected, these bumps will leave ugly dark scars on your face. Medicated soaps, creams and lotions will help dry up acne bumps as you clean. They have proved to help a skin once covered with sick-looking pimples. If you've been using regular cleansing creams and lotions . . . stop, at once! The oily base of normally formulated cleansing agents will slow up the healing process, and even make the condition of your skin worse. The seriousness of acne has made it possible to find an assortment of preparations in the drugstores or cosmetic counters that will help with the cure. Sulphur lotions are popular, and in many cases have worked successfully. Sulfur powder, purchased over the drug counter, mixed with a little butter or margarine into a smooth but dry paste, is a good old-fashioned remedy. A good wash-up is a must after it has been applied and allowed to dry. Follow up this treatment with a medicated lotion. If you wake up some morning and find that the bumps on your face are acne bumps, whatever you do . . . DON'T.

DON'T — WHATEVER YOU DO

DON'T cover up. Keep your face free. Let the sunshine and fresh air help to move away the bumps. DON'T select a hair style that covers the forehead or touches your face. The oil and dandruff from your hair will only irritate an already bad condition. DON'T skip shampoos. Your hair should be washed more frequently. A shampoo once a week is good if you can manage it. DON'T wear heavy mask-type makeup. You can't hide acne bumps, even if you try. These bumps have a way of pushing right through. They want to be seen. DON'T pick at your face. Digging and gouging with dirt-packed fingernails cause infections. This kind of picking at your face will leave marks that refuse to move later on. Then you're marked for life. DON'T drink soda pop and other carbonated drinks. Wait until your skin is well and smooth. DON'T forget your diet. It couldn't be more important than now. Chocolates, rich frostings, greasy pastries and fried, fatty foods should be left out of your daily diet. Make regular visits to your dentist and be absolutely sure you have no tooth trouble. If these pimples are serious enough for you to seek the advice of the doctor, follow his orders carefully and remember this care must be constant. Acne bumps will not disappear with on-and-off medication.

PERIOD PIMPLES

Don't confuse the "period pimple" with acne bumps. They just aren't the same. The period pimple is a hard under-the-surface bump. The acne bump bursts forth and sits on the surface of the skin. The period pimple is a warning that that time of the month is here again. This is a tricky bump. You never know when it's going to show up. It has a way of popping up after everything is all over. Whenever it does, it will vanish just as quickly and quietly as it appeared, if it is left alone. Like acne bumps, it too will leave its mark if picked at.

BLACKHEADS

There are some blackheads that just will not move by themselves. They need your help. But never, never, never use your fingernails on them. If blackheads reach the point of just being there, felt but not seen, they should be removed. With a cleansing tissue or soft cloth, cover the finger tips and press gently, but don't squeeze. This tender "pushing out" should not mark or mar your skin. When a bump is ready to move . . . it will. If it is not ready, it will not budge. Leave the stubborn ones and try again in another day or two. If they still refuse to move, apply a dab of cream or medicated ointment. Keep that area soft and soon it will be just right and will come out without too much forcing.

MAKEUP FOR ALL

Until recent years, makeup was something that teen girls bypassed. Some couldn't be so bothered, others were not allowed. It is still something that girls can take or leave alone. Most young girls like the addition of a little makeup. They feel undressed without it. Today even parents are more understanding about makeup and its use by the younger generation. Certain faces need more help than others, and makeup is supposed to do just that.

Some girls are guided by their age, and an early start in the makeup department is just a light application of lipstick. Others, a little more daring, might want to concentrate on the eyes, making this their outstanding facial feature. There's still another group that feels a good over-all makeup job is the answer to their facial beauty. Girls, today, are with it if they've learned to wear some makeup, even if it's just a little and only on weekends. You're real smart if you apply your makeup with light easy applications . . . producing a look that is natural . . . naturally you. Whether you are ready for makeup or not, there are steps to follow to produce a face of natural beauty. You may as well learn them now. When you're ready, the beginning will not be too difficult.

Think of your face as an artist's canvas . . . one that

is smooth and clean. As you begin to create a picture of beauty, take another hint from the artist. He begins with some general idea about the kind of picture he wants to create before he puts his brushes to work. The beauty world has given you almost as many brushes to work with. The softness of these brushes leave a "touched" unpainted look.

A FOUNDATION

Start with a foundation. Choose a color that is a good match to your skin tone. Smooth over the entire face and neck. A little rubbed over the lips and eyelids makes the finished job smoother. The experts use two or sometimes three shades of foundation to cover facial flaws. I wouldn't try any tricks, if I were you. Just play it natural, and remember, easy does it. Rouge is your next step. It adds a "blush" to your cheeks. Overlooking the use of rouge because of skin color is a big mistake. If rouge is used correctly, the slightest touch of color on the darkest skin will magnify the hidden color under the skin. Naturally if too much is used the under color is destroyed. Rouge should never be seen. Apply a light touch to the cheekbones. Blend carefully into the skin. Blushes add a gleam of color to your cheeks.

CHOOSE A POWDER

Face powder comes two ways: compressed in a cake, or loose in a box. The loose, most often, does the best job. With a clean cotton pad used for each application, the powder, matched to your skin, is patted and pressed all over the face and neck. With a beauty brush or another clean cotton ball, lightly brush away the excess. Compact or compressed powder is used for touch-up jobs. Beware of grimy powder puffs. They transfer facial germs and dirt from one spot to another. Keep a generous supply of cotton on hand to be used one time and one time only.

EYE BEAUTY

The next step is eye makeup. For girls your age, you don't have to get too serious with eyes that are already attractive. If your eyebrows are wild and unruly, a smoothing up job should be done before applying eyebrow pencil. Tweeze away stray hairs. Train them to stay in place with a little oil and a good brushing every other night until they are trained into the right shape. Never shape your eyebrows with a razor. Even very fine thin hairs can be removed with the tweezers. Do not destroy the natural line. If your eyebrows do not grow smooth and natural, short quick strokes with the eyebrow pencil will be all you'll need to easily shape them. Eye liner, eye shadow and mascara have recently gained their importance in the makeup field. All three can improve the shape and increase the size of your eyes. But this takes a lot of practice, which you really don't have time for now. Outlined eyes and exaggerated eyebrows are not for very young girls. If you've reached the dating age and something very special is in the works, remember eyes that sparkle are eyes that are interesting. They can hold a boy's attention for a long time. But if you're too young for eye glamour, stick with a light touch of Vaseline smoothed on your eyelids. Just that added tip of glitter will do wonders under soft lights and pale moonlight.

LIP COLOR

The last finishing touch is lipstick. Never before have we had so many colors to select from. However, you must wear a lipstick before you can really know what color it is going to be on you. Lipstick colors change. The color of skin and the lip color makes this possible. Your skin color may not take quick color changes. The smart thing to do is to find one good basic color that blends with your clothing and stick with it. Change gradually as you build up an assortment of lip colors.

You may never do anything more with your face but add a gentle touch of color to your lips. Lipstick is the most common and most used cosmetic. A little should be worn each day, even if only a touch of lip gloss, allowing your natural color to shine through. The application of lipstick should follow the shape of your mouth almost perfectly. Don't pull any tricks! Trying to change the shape of your lips with strokes of color outside or inside the natural line will only destroy the normal shape. Do not make up your lips to attract attention. Dusting them with face powder before using lipstick gives them a smooth and unpainted look. It locks in the color. If the spread of lipstick is smooth, it will remain secure and will not seep into dry cracks around the lip edges.

USE A LIP BRUSH

For a beautifully natural mouth, learn to use a lip brush. At first it will not be easy. Practice will make it perfect. Let the beauty representatives help you select a good lip brush. If the little fine hairs are not soft and blended together, the line you draw will not be smooth, but nervous and fuzzy. When you've practiced long enough and want to try your hand at it, get a good load of lipstick on the brush. With brush in hand, starting from the outer corner, outline the shape of the upper lip. Let the line extend slightly longer than the natural line of the lower lip. Outline the lower lip in the same way. Fill in the unpainted lips with color from the stick or with the brush. If applied this way, there will be no reason for blotting, because you have just enough color on your lips for a natural glow.

A CLEAN, NATURAL BEAUTY

If you feel you need to wear a complete makeup job each day, every particle must be washed and cleaned away at bed time. Stale makeup will quickly destroy a lovely smooth skin. Sleeping in make-up only means disaster for your skin. Makeup or no, some time each day must be given to clearing away dirt and dust that rests on the surface of the skin. It's even better if you can remove your makeup and reapply it. Adding to makeup during the day overloads the skin and the late date results are no longer the natural look you started with in the morning.

A face that exhibits natural beauty, even with makeup, is one that is truly lovely to see and admire. This is your face. Do with it what you please. Remember it is a face that can do wonderful things for you. You must be proud of it.

Do not copy makeup tricks, unless you know they will work for you, and that will only come with practice. Cosmetics are like your clothes. Wear those that look best on you. Copying from your friends may only bring terrifying results.

7

This Is Your Mouth

Your mouth is the most outstanding feature of your face. It must be attractive . . . inside and out. When you talk, the person to whom you speak looks directly at your mouth. It can express warmth, sincerity and self-confidence. It can also reflect shyness, hurt feelings or insecurity.

Your lips help you control your feelings. What happens when you get angry? With all your strength, you press your lips tightly together, and somehow that firmness helps you to get hold of yourself. Remember as a child when you wanted to cry and didn't want others to know that you were upset, and how you tried to hide your hurt feelings? Your lips began to quiver and before you knew it, tears were streaming down your cheeks. You felt better, and some of the hurt had gone. It's good, sometimes, to let go. But twisting and turning your mouth into strange, odd shapes at times while trying to hide your feelings becomes a bad habit and before you know it your mouth has lost its original beauty and shape. Since this is the center of interest on your face, you must do all you can to keep it attractive.

SEE YOUR DENTIST

Your lips may take on a perfect formation and the application of your lipstick may reveal the work of skillful hands, but making changes on the inside of your mouth is a job for the dentist. He not only does the every-six-month cleaning job that you cannot do, but will change the position of your teeth, if necessary. Just as the doctor keeps your body healthy, the dentist does the same for your mouth. If your mouth is unhealthy, it is unattractive.

When you smile, do you really smile? Is your laugh a good hearty one? Or are you afraid and ashamed to really let go, for fear others will see that the inside of your mouth has been overlooked in your good grooming routine? If you want to be heard, you can't talk with your lips held together. You can't laugh with your mouth closed. Keeping your lips together doesn't really hide anything . . . even bad breath. This little trick only gives you away. If your teeth are bright and clean, and your breath is fresh and clean-smelling, there should be no reason why you would not want to let go, open your mouth and speak with confidence and assurance. Please, whatever you do, don't let bad breath rob you of the pleasure of smiling prettily or laughing heartily.

If your beauty routine has been under good control, but you can't do much with your teeth other than daily cleaning, the dentist can. If your teeth are not perfectly placed, don't fret. You will not have to go through life with this deformity. The dentist can make near-perfect corrections. If you were marked with buck or protruding teeth as a child, it is true that then was the time to do something about putting them back into position. But you can do something about it now. It is never too late to make improvements. Any that make a better you are well worthwhile. If your teeth are not growing to please you, correct that now.

If you haven't already done so, find a good dentist. Get one on your own, use the one in school, go to the clinic or neighborhood hospital. If your tooth irregularity is beyond his control, he will recommend a specialist that handles only dental deformities. As an extra precaution, keep pencils, pens, matches, straight pins, bobby pins, toothpicks and all other such articles out of your mouth. Not only is this habit dangerous, but in time your teeth will be thrown out of line if it continues. These things can encourage mouth diseases.

A CLEAN HEALTHY MOUTH

Keeping your mouth clean and healthy is a never-ending job. It goes on and on for the rest of your life. You certainly want to keep your own teeth forever, if you can. Take it from me, if your mouth is not properly cared for and your teeth are left without early care, they won't be yours for long. You will be wearing store-bought teeth long before your time. So you can see that all the daily reminders to brush your teeth after each meal (when you can) and before going to bed are for your own good and the strength of your teeth. A thorough brushing twice a day is necessary for good strong teeth, but it will be to your advantage if you can manage a third. Whenever you do use your toothbrush, make sure you use it correctly.

BRUSHING YOUR TEETH

Like brushing your hair, there is a right way to brush your teeth. Brushing with an up and down motion, changing to a rotating motion now and then is the only way that each tooth gets a thorough cleaning job. The rotating motion will massage your gum line . . . essential to good strong teeth. Brushing and polishing the front of your teeth is not enough. The back must get the same attention. Your job is to remove the food particles that cling between your teeth. Remaining food frequently causes tooth decay, and this is why "after-meal-brushing" is so important.

If brushing is inconvenient after meals, washing your mouth can be beneficial. If done immediately, particles of food have not had time to get comfortably set and they can be washed away easily. Remember, this is only good if circumstances do not make brushing possible. Nothing can take the place of your toothbrush.

Seeing your dentist twice a year is a "must" on your list of things necessary for self-improvement. If the condition of your mouth makes it necessary for your trips to the dentist to be more frequent, let nothing interfere. Regular examinations allow your dentist to discover early decayed teeth, irregular growth and mouth disease. Early treatments can correct these conditions. Even pearly white and sparkling clean teeth need professional cleaning every six months. There are areas that your toothbrush tries to reach, but just can't. The instruments used by your dentist clean out every nook and cranny. This is one of his important jobs in caring for your teeth. Depending on your individual needs, your dentist may recommend a different brushing method. He will know what is best for your teeth. Pay close attention to your teeth and their growth. If you notice any changes discuss them with your dentist. Follow his advice and you'll have good teeth for a long time.

DIET MAKES STRONG TEETH

Weak, unhealthy teeth may be due to diet deficiency. Strong healthy teeth depend on the foods you eat. So again, the importance of your diet is strongly emphasized. You're only kidding yourself if you think you can eat all the wrong foods or skip meals completely and not have trouble inside your mouth. It may not be noticeable immediately, but have no fear, it will show up sooner or later. Sweets are promoters of tooth decay. Don't be one of those girls who is always nibbling on a chocolate bar. Nibble on something more nutritious instead. If you drink enough milk, eat plenty of fresh vegetables and fruit, eggs, cheese and butter, it is not likely you will have this inside trouble. A diet suggestion may come from your dentist. He may want you to have more or less of certain foods. He has this right. Follow his orders.

Foods like nuts, hard rolls, toasted bread, raw fruits and vegetables require harder chewing. These foods help develop strong gums; the chewing is good exercise for your teeth. It has been said that the fibers of fresh oranges, celery and other stringy foods have positive cleaning value. In general, a good diet is essential for healthy attractive teeth.

BAD BREATH

There's a strange thing about bad breath. If you have it, even your best friend wouldn't dare mention it to you. She will talk about it to others. It is caused by many things; you can't be too careful. One of the main reasons for bad breath is mouth neglect. Another is, again, diet. And still another is highly scented spicy foods. Some people can eat foods with high flavor and spice and their breath is not affected. In other cases the same foods may leave a definite mark of unpleasantness. Like other things, bad breath can be a clue to something wrong inside. Cavities in the teeth and infections in the mouth are some other reasons for bad breath. Mild mouth washes, used as often as is necessary, will help you combat this unpleasantness. If the odor gets out of hand, check with the dentist or the doctor.

It is true that hundreds of mouth washes are to be found at any one of your favorite drug counters and discount stores. Rinsing your mouth with a baking soda and salt water mixture will ease bad breath, when you don't have anything else. It's good to know that the salt tightens your gums. If, in the beginning, you are not too sure about what to buy and use, purchase a small amount of a product that looks interesting, and try it. If your mouth doesn't like the taste, or if you get tired of the same flavor, try another. Most mouth washes will at least add temporary freshness to bad breath.

8

These Are Your Hands

A perfect appearance is one that is neat and trim right down to the tips of your fingers.

Did you ever realize how really necessary your hands are? They move as you talk to express your thoughts. You raise them in the classroom when you want attention. They open and shut doors. They carry your belongings. They touch things and people to make them more meaningful to you. They hold the hand of someone you like. They make contact with another when shaking hands. They add warmth and comfort to a friend with a serious problem. They do all the "personal" work to make you more attractive. If you and I wanted to take the time, there would be no end to the long list of the many wonderful things our hands do for us.

YOUR HANDS ARE IN THE
SPOTLIGHT

With not too much thought at all, we do know that our hands are always in the spotlight. Even if you wanted to, you couldn't hide them. They are always right "out there" to be seen. Can yours afford this spotlight treatment? Do they make a good impression for you? Are you proud of them? Do you use them with self-assurance? Or are you ashamed of how they look?

You and your girl friends sit around and talk about many things. Seldom does the talk circle around your hands and their care. You may not talk about them, but they talk for you and talk about you. Have you ever, just for "kicks," had your palm read? The fortuneteller looks into your future (so she says) just by looking at your two hands. Your whole life is right there, she tells you. You may not believe in such things, but the secrets about your grooming habits, your general health, your mental state and your personality are all revealed by the way your hands look and the way you use them. It is said that hands can tell your age quicker than the lines in your face. Hands, like the rest of you, go through changes. As you get older, so do they. It's a terrible shock to have your hands looking older than your years. If your hands are "forgotten," and not taken care of, they may grow old before you. What girl wants this?

HANDS EXPRESS FRIENDLINESS

A person to whom you are being introduced may look you dead in the eye, not saying one word. The feel of your hand tells some of the story about you. It is right there that the direct contact is made. From your own experience, you know what an empty feeling you were left with when you shook a lifeless hand. There's nothing worse! And there's nothing better than one that's warm and friendly . . . a handshake that is firm and confident. Even if you'd like to, you can't very well hide the story your hands will tell about you. So if you want the real story told, this requires the proper hand and nail care. Pretty, healthy fingernails just don't happen. They demand daily attention. Even if you've neglected yours, there's still time to make early corrections, starting now. If your hands are already well-kept and attractive, it just means that you know the importance of good grooming . . . from head to toe, and stopping now and then at your finger tips.

Anyway you take it, the first important rule in hand care, like everything else, is cleanliness. Your hands must be washed several times a day. Your hands carry germs. How many times a day do you touch your face? Your ears? Your lips? You probably couldn't even count the times you rub your eyes with your finger tips. These are very delicate areas, easily irritated by the touch of dirty hands.

NAIL POLISH DOES NOT COVER UP NEGLECT

There is more to pretty hands than bright colored nail polish. Nail polish has been a life saver for many of us. But spreading bright polish on broken, split, uncared-for, dirty fingernails doesn't hide or cover up neglect. Hands that are clean and fingernails that are unbitten, with a healthy protected look, do not need polish to make them attractive. The use of fingernail polish is only a matter of personal taste. A little touch of color at your fingertips will add glamour to your hands and their appearance. But yours can be just as lovely and attractive without it. Since you already know that your personal beauty must be extended right down to the tip of your fingers, you'd be unfair to yourself to allow broken fingernails and neglected hands destroy all the good things you have going for yourself. If your hands are badly in need of repair, start today to make the necessary corrections.

Even healthy, attractive hands must be washed several times a day. Start with warm water and lots of good soap suds. Loosen fingernail dirt with a nail brush, if you have one (if not, add it to your Christmas list). This little brush is good for cleaning up dirty, discolored knuckles. Massage these joints as you soap and scrub. Rinse well until all soap disappears. Dry thoroughly. After each washing, with the tip of your towel, push back the softened cuticle. Apply hand lotion, drop one or two of oil or petroleum jelly. Work well into the areas where it is need d most. Lotions and creams keep your hands soft and add moisture to dry, rough hands. All this makes your manicuring job so much easier.

HAVE THE PROPER TOOL TO GET THE JOB DONE

Some time must be devoted to a weekly manicure. If you've never given yourself one, you'll need some practice. You can't do a very good job if you don't have the necessary equipment. These tools need not upset your budget. Put aside a few cents weekly and you can afford them. Here are some of the things you will need.

1. nail brush
2. towel (hand size; clean)
3. absorbent cotton
4. emery boards
5. orange stick
6. oily cuticle remover
7. nail clippers (if you know how to use them)
8. polish remover
9. fingernail polish
10. liquid base coat
11. liquid top coat
12. hand lotion

SELECT A TIME FOR WEEKLY NAIL CARE

When you get everything in order, select a time for manicuring when you will not be disturbed and rushed. Following your bath or right after doing the dishes is excellent. Your nails have had a good chance to soak, the cuticle has been softened and the dirt under the nails can be easily moved.

Take the polish first. If you wear it, remove it. Cover each nail with a small piece of cotton, moistened with polish remover. Allowed to stay put for a moment, the soaked cotton softens the polish and with one stroke, from base of nail to tip, nail polish disappears like magic. Cream nail polish remover is easy to use and conditions the nail as it removes stale polish. Each day, if you look, you will find new methods for making everything easy. Select the method that is best for you and your budget.

Shape your nail to a nice oval with an emery board. Insert the emery board to fit under the nail edge and keep it slightly slanted. (Your nail is apt to split if the emery board is placed more to the top of nail.) Move from side to center of the nail with one-direction strokes. Do not saw! Do not cut deep into the flesh. With short quick strokes shape the nail as you desire, without points. Recheck for rough edges.

Cuticle oil or cream is then applied, when shaping is complete on one hand. Shape the other hand. Apply oil or cream.

Soak your fingers in warm soapy water. Dry thoroughly. Remove all moisture between flesh and nail.

An orange stick, used on the blunt end, is wrapped with cotton, dampened slightly with cuticle oil. Gently push back the cuticle. Run the covered stick under your fingernail to soften and remove the dirt. Change the cotton as often as necessary.

Scrub your nails when they are returned to soapy water. Use the nail brush to remove oil and any loose cuticle. Rinse in clear water. Dry each nail with the end of your towel. Again, push the cuticle back and remove any dead skin or sharp nail edges. Use nail clippers, but only if you've had lots of practice. Oil applications, between manicures, remove cuticles in a flash. Nippers are not necessary if cuticles are given daily care.

Apply base coat. This is your nail protector. Even if you do not prefer colored polish, a thin base coat brushed lightly over the entire nail adds brightness and protects the nail from discoloration. When the base coat is thoroughly dry, apply the first coat of nail polish. If necessary, apply a second coat when the first application is dry.

A top coat is applied after the polish is thoroughly dry. This insures longer protection and the nail polish will not streak. A thin coat of sealer can be applied daily . . . giving added protection and a newness to your manicure.

When your nails are all dry, dab cuticle oil around the cuticle of each nail. Massage gently around the nail with finger tips. Blot surplus oil with tissue.

With hand lotion or cream applied to the back of the hands, massage well by rubbing the two backs together. This is where the moisture and oil is needed most. In the end, rub your two palms together, massaging as you blend hand lotion or oil into the skin. Here are hands you will be proud of and hands you can extend with pride and confidence.

HELPING HINTS FOR HANDSOME HANDS

Since nail polish gets the most attention and there are so many colors to choose from, be careful when you make your selection. The color of your hands will give you some clues. Think of polish as you do the color of your lipstick you use. It must enhance the color of your skin . . . make it alive and more beautiful. Lipstick and fingernail polish do not have to match, but they must blend and harmonize.

Nail hardeners have a touch of color. When they are used the polish is not necessary. Test all products for yourself that say they will do unusual jobs. Some can be more harmful than helpful. If you pick any one of the products to harden the nails or make them grow, apply first to only one finger. Keep a close watch for a few days. If the nail continues to look "normal," the product is safe for you to use. Read the directions carefully. Keep your fingers away from your eyes.

If you are a polish-user and wear it most of the time, every now and then let your nails go unpolished for a few days, after your manicure. Used too frequently, nail polish can be drying, and the natural oil is removed from the nail. Soak your fingers in warm olive oil a few times a month. If your nails peel and you have cuticle trouble, this is a good helpmate to get them strong and healthy again. Another good remedy is a dab or two of oil at bedtime. Rub into the corners and around the finger tips. A further suggestion to help polish stay in place longer is to rub vinegar on each nail before applying the polish. Try it, for it works!

If you are a polish-picker, give up this bad habit. Fingernail polish must be either all on or all off.

Between manicures, lemon juice will aid in removing dark spots on knuckles and finger edges. Rub on affected areas or over the entire hand after each washing. A few drops of peroxide in water when you give yourself a weekly manicure will remove discoloration from your nails and finger tips. If either is used, they bleach out and dry the skin, so heavier use of cream or oil is necessary.

Hangnails can be hazardous. When they appear, remove immediately before they tear down the nail base and tear up precious nylons.

For hands that perspire—and they will if you're nervous—use an anti-perspirant two or three times a week, rubbed right into the palm of your hands or pat a drop or two of alcohol in your hands until all moisture disappears.

Pumice stone works effectively when used on stubborn hand bumps and calluses. These rough spots can also be rubbed away with a mixture of pumice powder and cream or oil. Rub the affected spots and remove with soap and water. Smooth out any roughness with a generous helping of hand cream or lotion.

Sleeping in gloves may sound wild and crazy, but if your nails are extra bad and your hands need all the care you can give them, then it makes good sense. Sheer, thin gloves, made of cheese cloth, are good for sleeping. They can be purchased in the drug store. Hang on to old summer cotton gloves and use them. They do the same trick. Rub each finger with oil. The gloves keep the oil in place, giving it a chance to work while you sleep.

Finger nails are not for removing staples, opening bottles and jars and untying hard-to-undo-knots.

Keep your hands soft and lovely. Carry your own soap. Liquid soap in public places removes the natural oil and moisture from your hands, leaving them dry and rough.

Unhealthy nails that peel, break and split can be greatly helped by a daily dose of gelatine. It now comes flavored and is a delight to take. If you don't like the mixing, try a tablet with no taste at all. Gelatine will clear up nail problems within a few months.

Protect your hands from extremely cold weather. Cover them with gloves or mittens when the winter months demand it.

Also cover them with household gloves (another way to use up old, discarded cotton or nylon ones) when doing your chores. This is good protection from bending and breaking nails. If you're one of those girls that just can't wear gloves, rub your nails over a wet cake of soap for additional protection against snapping and breaking.

Nail biting is against the law of good grooming. Boys

don't like girls who chew their nails down to a nub; they don't like long claw-like fingernails, either. If nail chewing is a habit you think you can't break, paint your nails with a stinging, bitter-tasting medicine. This should keep your fingers out of your mouth.

ELBOWS ON DISPLAY

Elbows are one of the most forgotten parts of your body. If you include them in your hand care program, and give them added attention at bath time, they will soon begin to look better.

Just because you don't see them, unless your attention is called to how horrible they look, don't think they are hidden from the eyes of others. Everybody, but everybody sees them. Elbows take a beating. They work hard for you, whether you know it or not. They are banged on table and desk tops, you bump and knock them on heaven knows what, and yet you neglect them. They belong to the rest of your body, but they dangle there looking as if they belonged somewhere else. Most of the time they go all winter long with no care. But when summer comes, they are expected to come right out in the open looking smooth and beautiful. If they are rough and discolored, you dread getting into sleeveless, low cut dresses. If they've been allowed to go along by themselves for a long time, don't expect them to make overnight changes with the first little bit of summer treatment they get. Just like your hands, they too must get some daily attention. You can make their appearance brighter by scrubbing them during your daily bath and as often as you can when you wash your hands. They'll be much cleaner and smoother.

Your bath brush or washcloth and lots of soap and good scrubbing will help loosen the hard dirty skin that causes elbow discoloration. Remove all the soap, rub

briskly when drying and soften up with baby oil, cream
or lotion.

CITRUS FRUITS FOR BLEACHING

Be thrifty and use everything to its fullest. Did you ever
think of trying used halves of lemon or grapefruit? They
do a great bleaching job. Sit with your elbows right into
the center of either and stay put for a while. This is a
good time to study or catch up on your reading. The fruit
may be left over from the breakfast or dinner table, but
there's plenty of acid still left deep down inside. The acid
down near the core does a better bleaching job than soap
and water will do. Rinse well after this citrus soaking,
then apply cream or lotion to the treated area.

Using a dry pumice stone is another good elbow
smoother. For good results try this treatment before
going to bed. Rub your elbows lightly to remove the dead,
dry dark skin. Apply lubrication. Let remain overnight.
While you're sleeping, it will do a super softening-up job.
Repeat this treatment two or three times a week. Follow
these simple rules and your elbows will be smooth
enough to become another beauty asset. In no time you'll
be proud and not ashamed of yours.

9

These Are Your Feet

The average person will walk approximately 70,000 miles in a lifetime, so the experts say. If your feet ever hurt, really hurt, your entire body is in pain. This is an experience that is not quickly forgotten. If this has happened to you more than once, then it is high time you did something about relieving yourself of such misery. Hurting feet do horrible things to your body. Foot aches and pains destroy graceful body motions, play havoc with your posture, not to mention what these pains will do to your disposition. Ugly lines and wrinkles appear in your face, and you're hard to get along with.

Your feet are so important to the rest of your body. Where could you go without them? They take so much abuse and get no rewards. Constant neglect is the main reason for people going through life with hurting feet. Feet can be ruined if they don't get some care and attention. Why wait for them to cry out in pain for your attention?

KEEP YOUR FEET IN GOOD CONDITION

The care of your feet should be an important part of your personal care program. If you start now to keep them in good condition, they are apt to give you good service for a long, long time. Don't make the mistake that many girls do. Don't wait until your feet start to hurt, day after day. When they start to give you this kind of trouble, and you can't take it any longer, then you want to do something about it. Sometimes it's too late. As good as your feet are to you, they deserve just as much pampering and petting as your hands and face. They are precious and the more kindness they get from you, the longer you can eliminate foot troubles. Like everything else, if they are disregarded now, they will grow into major problems later on as you grow older.

Why do feet hurt, anyway? The list of reasons is long. The two most common causes are excessive strain on your feet and ill-fitting shoes. Remember that old saying, "If the shoe fits, wear it." A good addition might have been, "and if it doesn't, leave it where you found it." Nothing can ruin your feet quicker than shoes that don't fit. Shoes that are too short, stockings and socks that are too small, cramp your feet. Naturally this causes bad walking habits, promotes leg cramps, interferes with circulation and makes calluses, corns and bunions. But no matter how bad the trouble is, it can probably be corrected. Even flat feet or fallen arches can be corrected if looked after early enough. It has been frequently said, that these two foot problems are common to people of dark skins. This may or may not be true, but I've seen a lot of bad feet in my day; the majority were all due to neglect, and color of skin had nothing to do with it.

YOUNG FEET

Don't think for one minute that your feet are too young to be looked after. Keep a close watch on them; start now to take care of strange bumps and bones—large or small— that become noticeable. If they are seen in spots where they never appeared before, do something about getting them back into place. The only way you can go through life with a happy smile on your face is to have happy feet free of pain. Don't spend all your time on your face, neglecting your feet. Your face is at least exposed to the fresh air and sunlight. But your poor feet are closed in and cooped up in shoes and stockings and rarely get such a treat. Have you noticed how they wiggle and squirm once they are free? Expose them as often as you can. They love the feeling of freedom when you walk around without shoes. They thrive on walking on the bare ground. They like the feeling of the moisture of the earth and the softness of the beaches in the summer. They are equally as happy when they can feel the bare floor or the softness of the carpet when they are indoors. Too many girls are embarrassed when the time comes to show off their feet. No matter how good you look in your skimpy, bared bathing suit, ugly, uncared-for feet are unflattering. Don't let your feet be the reason for not getting out with the crowd when summer comes again. Prepare them now for outdoor exposure.

IF THE SHOE FITS—WEAR IT

One of the first things to remember when caring for your feet is to get the right kind and the right size shoe. Not the size you wore the last time you bought a pair of shoes, because you probably won't be wearing the same size. You're still growing and your feet are still developing

Statistics show that eighty per cent of the American public suffer from some type of foot disability during their lifetime. The percentage of women sufferers is much larger than men. A leader in this field says that, "The weaker sex fit their eyes rather than their feet."

Everyday shoes that are too soft and too comfortable, with no foot support, make trouble when the weekend rolls around. All week you've allowed your feet to spread "all over the place" and on Sunday you try to squeeze them into your "Sunday best" shoes. What a time you have! You wouldn't have this trouble if you selected everyday shoes properly constructed for comfort and protection. Tennis shoes, soft fabric shoes, flat loafers with little or no inner-construction are bad for your feet, especially if they are worn every day. You will find today that most tennis shoes and loafer-type soft shoes are built with some inner support. These are the best for your feet. They will cost a little more than the others, but the investment will be a good one. Your feet will be happy and easy to get along with for a longer time.

When you buy shoes always have your foot measured. Don't tell the salesman what size you wear, let him tell you. Don't be guilty of falling madly in love with one style, and no matter what, you just must have it. The salesman may tell you that he doesn't have that shoe in your size and you insist he bring out the nearest thing to it. You squeeze your foot into it, and before you allow him to speak, you tell him they are comfortable. "They are a little tight, and they do pinch a wee bit," you whisper softly to yourself. You continue to convince yourself that with a little "breaking in" they'll be a perfect fit. Away you go out of the shoe store, with your shoe box tucked neatly under your arm. But who's sorry now? Not the salesman. He made the sale and hopes he never sees you again. Where does this leave you? With shoes that are harmful to your feet and give you discomfort every time you wear them. Nine times out of ten you are never able to live through the misery of breaking them in.

When buying your shoes, remember that they must fit your foot. Fit them properly! Make sure they don't bind or cut. The shoe should be snug but not tight, with a little space between your toes and the tip of the shoe. The widest part of your foot should fit the wide part of your shoe. The heel of the shoes should mold itself to the heel of your foot without cutting. Bumps and calluses come from shoes that move up and down on your foot. A shoe that is too large is just as harmful to your foot as one that is too small.

TAKE A WALK AND A LONG LOOK

Shoe stores are nicely carpeted for your convenience. Plenty of space has been provided for you to walk around in so you can be assured of foot comfort before your purchase is made. Take a good long walk. Your foot can be as much as a whole shoe size smaller when you're sitting down as when you're standing up. Take your time in making your selection. Don't let the salesman or a friend shopping with you rush you into buying your shoes. This is one purchase, above all the rest, that requires long concentration. Know what you want in a shoe. Know what demands you will place on it.

Beware of foot fads. Just because everybody else is wearing something, doesn't mean that you have to be one of the crowd. If your shoe wardrobe is well stocked with the right kind of shoes, mule-type and fancy open-work shoes may be considered—but only if you promise to wear them at the right time and for the right occasion. Even when the right occasion comes along, there are often too many feet shoved into open shoes that are at least a half size too small. Heels never looked so fat and ugly as when they hang over the back of bare shoes. The shoe-store owners are generous with mirrors. Use them! That's what they are there for. If your heels are flabby and fat, they would rather not be out in the open. They would like it better, and so will you, if they could snuggle neatly and comfortably into a closed heel shoe.

PROTECT YOUR FOOT COMFORT

Play it smart, protect your safety and insure yourself of foot comfort by selecting a simply styled shoe with low to medium heels. A plain shoe, even if it's the only one in your wardrobe, with care, will take you many places and will always be ready when duty calls. If your shoes fit, you can wear them gracefully with confidence and poise. Knowing that the fit is right, it's up to you to keep your feet in good condition. A little care each day and a thorough self-examination once a week is required . . . this once-a-week check will mean clipping, cutting, pushing cuticle, oiling and massaging—just the care you give your hands.

A WEEKLY PEDICURE

Right after your bath is a good time to take care of your feet. The rough dry spots have had a chance to soften up, making them easier to remove. Dry callused places can mean later trouble and mar the beauty of your feet. With a little elbow grease and a damp pumice stone, dead surface skin can be removed once or maybe twice a week. At bath time, try massaging your leg muscles right down to your ankles. Work up a good circulation. Foot strain will be removed and leg tiredness and tension will be relieved. Your toes should get a good lubrication job and cuticles need careful attention. If neglected, cuticles become hard and dry, making them more difficult to push back. If you find them stubborn, try wrapping a cotton compress soaked in oil around each toe. Let stand for a minute or two. The oil will soften the toenail and the cuticle will move into place easily. Any ridges that appear on the nail surface can be smoothed away with gentle strokes with your emery board.

Shape your toenails with nail clippers or manicuring scissors in straight-across fashion. Careful now! Don't cut deep into the corners. Deep cuts encourage ingrown toenails. Smooth the rough edges of the nail with an emery board. Never use a fingernail file. If you like color, by all means apply polish to your toenails. The same method is used as in manicuring your fingernails. The polish starts from the base of the nail and continues right out to the tip with long even strokes.

For feet that have had a good workout during the day, give them special soaking at night. For soothing cool results alternate between warm water and almost cold. Rub your feet with cream, oil or hand lotion. Better still, if you're heading for bed, pat them with your favorite cologne and dust them with talcum powder. You'll sleep like a lamb and your feet will take wings the next day.

Check the list of "Foot Facts" below and keep your feet comfortable and healthy.

FOOT FACTS

Put on clean socks or stockings every day.

Make sure that the fit is right. It's as important as the fit of your shoe. Too-tight stockings or socks are harmful to your feet and deprive you of a graceful walk.

Perspiring feet must be washed frequently. Medicated foot powder or ordinary talcum will reduce perspiration and ward off unpleasant foot odors.

If foot perspiration persists, stockings or socks must be changed at midday. Damp feet and wet footwear encourage blisters that can injure your feet.

Keep hardened heel bumps soft and lubricated, by taping on small squares of cotton soaked in oil or cream. Let stand for a few minutes. All dry, hard skin can now be easily removed with your pumice stone.

For feet that work hard, change your shoes the first chance you get. When possible relax them by getting into a slanting position—flat on your back with your feet at an angle higher than your head. Just ten minutes of this will make you feel like a million.

A once-a-week pedicure is essential; but use caution. Painful foot trouble can be caused by careless pedicures.

Don't fool around with razor blades. If stubborn corns and calluses cause foot pains, see your podiatrist, don't try to remove them yourself.

Keep your feet pretty and flexible with exercises and massage. Exercises increase circulation and are relaxing.

If you desire polish on your toenails, it does not have to match your fingernails perfectly, but it should harmonize.

It's a good idea to have two pairs of everyday shoes. Shoes worn a full day need about the same number of hours to air and dry out.

Everyday shoes must be sturdy enough to take hard wear. Make sure that every shoe you buy is constructed properly for comfort and support.

Chances are that shoes that have to be "broken in" will never feel good on your feet. Don't gamble on your feet! You can't afford the loss.

Shoe friction causes corns and calluses. Properly fitted shoes will prevent them.

Foot comfort is as easy as "pushing a button." New types of soothing foot sprays are plentiful.

LEG GROOMING

You haven't got a leg to stand on, if it is not as carefully cared for as your feet. Because of the rise and fall of skirts the importance of leg grooming has moved into number-one position. Where skirts start or stop is not important, but good grooming for your legs is.

Legs look more attractive when they are free of thick-growing hair. A slight fuzz may be all that shows now, but as you grow older, it will continue to grow. Once you decide to remove the hair from your legs, you'll probably have to keep it up. It's debatable that it will grow back thicker. If you shave the hairs away the removable job must be more frequent. If you've reached the stage where the hair detracts from your attractiveness, you don't want it. But unless the growth is heavy and thick, there's no reason for you to be concerned about removing it now. In Chapter 3 we discussed the various methods for removing unwanted hair. You will find directions there.

After every hair has been removed, give your legs a good washing. Dry well and rub gently with oil, Vaseline or lotion.

Your legs look more attractive when they are free of hair and cared for this way with lotion, oil or cream. Start this habit today!

COLOR IS IMPORTANT

Most girls have a wardrobe of stockings and socks. That's how important they are to fashion and a well groomed wardrobe. Not too long ago, if a girl owned one or two pairs of nylons, she was lucky . . . very lucky. Then, they were tucked away in a safe place, just waiting for some special occasion to come along. The rough, patterned, textured socks and stockings come in all colors to match or blend with any clothing color. You could almost, with your eyes closed, put your hands on one of these textured casuals and it would be right for daytime wear. But when it comes to selecting the sheers for dressier attire, you must be careful about the color you choose. You will want a color and weight to make your legs more attractive. This is just as important as the selection of the right coat or dress.

Nine pairs of brown legs out of ten, wear the wrong shade of hosiery. They insist on wearing dark unattractive stockings just because they think their brown skins demand it. This isn't so!

It is agreed that hosiery a trifle darker than the skin acts as a "slimmer" for legs that are a little on the fat side. Your legs, uncovered or covered, must look as if they belong to the rest of you. Dark, unattractive hosiery will only make dark legs darker and they do nothing to change the shape of the leg. It would be difficult to set a rule for dark skins to follow in the selection of hosiery colors. Our skin tones vary from very light to very dark. All our skins have undertones of pink, yellow, red or brown. You can readily understand why a rule cannot be established. It is important, when selecting a hosiery shade for yourself, to remember that the color you choose should not cover up the color of your legs, but enhance your leg beauty. Choose carefully when making your hosiery purchases. Try for a color that will give your legs a cosmetic look—the look you have given your face. Test the color by looking through its sheerness over the back of your hand, not forgetting that even on your legs you may not get that exact color.

From season to season hosiery colors change . . . moving from light to dark. More dramatic changes have been from white to dark colors, such as navy blue and black. It came as a surprise to many to see dark legs in white stockings. But those dark legs were just as smart and fashionable as those of lighter hues. The under-color of the legs look so much better when a soft glittering look peeps through. A sweep of oil or cream will you achieve this shimmer through already sheer nylons.

SOCKS AND STOCKINGS

Stockings with seams, called "full fashioned," are hard to come by in these days of seamless hoisery. Early in the beginning of nylon hosiery, this was the only style. As in every other industry, there have been some changes made. The smooth seamless stocking is hitting high on the fashion popularity list, and this is what most girls own.

If you know your legs look best with a seam (which makes them look smaller), start the search, and you'll find it. Every big department store includes stockings with a seam. The center line breaks the width of the heaviest part of your leg. If the seam is straight it adds beauty to the appearance of the legs. Don't be lazy and resort to seamless hosiery just to relieve yourself of the job of keeping seams straight, unless you are downright sure your legs need a smooth undivided look. Stockings without seams are good for thin legs. They make skinny legs look larger.

With very thin legs, you must be careful that stockings cling and fit. Stockings and socks, textured with patterns or smooth as silk, must give your legs proper support. Baggy stockings draw everyone's attention. You'd rather all eyes went the other way when your legs are not in perfect condition. To avoid this, wear a panty girdle or garter belt. There are some stockings that stay up without help. Stretch is everywhere and in most things we wear. Stockings have not been left out of the stretch of things. Those with stretchability cling and stay put all the time they're on your legs. The panty stockings are even better when it comes to staying up. Perfect fit is necessary for comfort.

If you're still wearing garters, check the strength of the

elastic. Garters that are too tight slow up the blood circulation, and leave dark marks on your legs. Heavy fat legs suffer more than thin ones. Stockings comes in three lengths . . . long, medium and regular. For little girls, the petite size is better than any.

Very young girls wear stockings now. A girl no longer has to wait for that certain age to feel "grown up" enough for stockings. Some even wear stockings and socks at the same time to create a "look." Others use double duty hosiery for protection from the cold. Knee socks over sheer nylons give just the finish some girls want.

Owning more leg fashions doesn't mean that you can ease up on keeping them all clean. Stockings and socks must be washed after each wearing, even if you don't want to use them again for another day or two. Clean stockings and socks are more healthy for your feet. You can't afford to be lazy when it comes to having beautiful feet and legs. More than ever, all eyes are on legs, and the prettier they are the better.

This Is Your Personality

Do you realize you're almost over the hump? You've come more than half way. Together, we've covered you from tip to toe. Any part of you we've left untouched, you might want to handle without help. But let's stick it out, because there's still more to do. The real foundation for all we've talked about can only work with those subjects we have yet to cover. One of the first is your poise and personality.

What is personality and how does it work? The definition of personality is very simple. One source says it is the sum total and organization of mental and physical traits and processes . . . some original and some acquired. Another believes that personality is made up of all your traits and tendencies, their balance and relation, their expression and their reaction on others. Still another says it is the sum total of traits that are necessary to describe what is to be one person. That person, in this

case, is YOU! Simply, personality is individual character
. . . *your* individual character. Personality is self-expres-
sion—the way you talk, the way you walk, everything you
say and do. Your good and bad habits as well as the way
you act and express yourself in relation to others adds up
to your personality.

A girl with all the beauty in the world can be lonely
and unhappy, if she is without friends. Your personality
depends on the kind of person you are. The kind of
person you are depends on your personality (if that's not
too hard to figure out). Your actions speak out for you.
They say how much or how little you are liked by others.
Now, don't say you don't care if others don't like you.
That's kid stuff, and you're only fooling yourself.
Whether you admit it or not, you can't really be happy if
you are disliked by those you come in contact with. It's
great if most people like you, but no matter how hard you
try, some won't like you at all. Their feeling about you
may never change. Don't waste time trying to change just
one person; there are too many others to fill that vacant
spot.

YOU ARE A SALESMAN

Since personality can be one of your biggest assets, why
not think of it as a product you are "showing off" and
"selling." However, it must be attractive to be seen and
admired. The way you handle yourself is what makes
people like and want to be with you. If you don't have
enough personality to help you do the things you want to
do, you're in trouble. You can't sell what you haven't got.
If this is your case, you have work to do.

If you have any knowledge of business, then you know
that a regular inventory check is one that reveals an
accurate account of the merchandise on hand. Those in
charge know at a glance what additional merchandise is

needed to continue the operation. The same method can be applied to you in developing your personality. Here is your first step. Make two lists, one listing your good habits and the other listing the bad. The first list will fill up in a hurry, but it will take some time to get the second one started. It's always easy finding fault with others, but it's another story when you think about your own. If you're honest with yourself, however, you know the kind of person you are. You know very well the things you do and say that make others like or dislike you. The things you dislike in yourself usually are outstanding enough for those around you to dislike, too. If you are accurate with your personality listing, you will be able to see your good points right away. This will give you great satisfaction, finding out just where you stand and how far you can go from here. If your self-evaluation is good, you can go far.

TAKE A LOOK AT YOU

At your age, it should be easy for you to make changes in your daily habits. For some it is, and for others it isn't easy at all. How can it be, when one day you like yourself and the next you don't? One day you're right there, in the middle of things, with everyone thinking you're the greatest. The next, for no good reason you can think of, you're overlooked completely. This "shakes" you up. You know your grades are good and you are just as attractive as the next girl. All these things are in your favor. You can't put your finger on what you're doing wrong—but it may be your personality. You may think you rate high in the personality department, but your friends don't think so at all. As long as your rating stays down, you'll be left out of things. Your good grades won't mean anything and your good looks even less. How does one know what habits to keep and which ones to get rid of? Checking the habits of others is one good way to start.

YOUR FRIENDS

Start with your friends. Watch all the things they do. Listen to what they have to say. Check their bad habits. Look at their good ones. Naturally, you like or dislike people for many reasons. They are normal reasons and they help you with your own self-evaluation. You can quickly think of reasons why some people don't get along well with others, but you can never understand when it happens to you. You see, what you do, what you say and how you think makes you different from other people. You are different. Your pattern of living is different. Your standards are different. You know you are not perfect. No one is. Getting a head start on perfecting some of your bad habits will take a little doing, at first. Making the decision to change is important. In fact it is necessary in these days of modern progress. True, you set your own standards for living, but when you are faced with choosing a career of your interest, standards will be set for you. You must measure up to be a success.

You've made errors. You will make others. There is no reason wasting time regretting or explaining all the wrong things you did yesterday. Make the personality changes and make the best of today. As you make these changes, you will dislike some people and others you will like a lot. No matter how much you like the good habits of the latter, don't copy them. Many times you may have wanted to be just like one of your favorite friends. Everyone has a friend somewhere that she wants to be like. You can be an all time favorite, too, liked by just as many people as the next fellow, without copying the personality of others. It's natural, however, for you to wonder why some of your friends seem to "have everything it takes." Think about one of your friends . . . one you admire. As far as you can see, she can do no wrong.

CHECK THEIR GOOD AND BAD HABITS

Why is she so well liked? Is it because she wants to be a part of the school activities and you always get lost in the shuffle? Is it because she is interested in what is happening around her, and you just take life for granted? Is it because she takes advantage of every moment in every day, and you go on from day to day not caring much about anything? Is it because she can make decisions for herself, and you still depend on someone to make them for you? Is it because she goes out of her way to be friendly and help others, and you are too concerned about yourself? Is it because she avoids gossiping groups and you're always in the middle of them?

Is it because she follows through on jobs that are given her, and you give up once things don't go the way you want them to? Is it because she can control her feelings and emotions and you fly off the handle at the least little thing? Is it because she takes criticism gracefully and you're ready to "let 'em have it" when you've been criticized? Is it because she can adapt herself to changes and you're lost when placed in a new situation? Is it because she is always willing to do more than her share and you always "pass the buck"? Is it because she will share the spotlight with others and you always "hog" the show?

Is it because she can take disappointments in her stride and you are "fit to be tied" when things go wrong? Is it because she has the ability to draw people to her and they seem to shy away from you? Is it because she is enthusiastic about the progress of others and you want to be the only one to get ahead? Is it because she is an interested listener as well as speaker and you talk all the time never giving the other fellow a chance? Is it because she is kind and courteous to older people and you don't have time to be bothered?

Is it because she always has time to love, respect and understand her family (and hope they understand her), and you rant and rave, bark and snap at yours, never trying to understand anything . . . or anybody? Is it because she never forgets to be a "lady" and you think it's cute to be everything but? Is it because she doesn't allow herself to be led astray and do things she knows are wrong and you think you must "follow the leader" (to have friends), not knowing where it will lead you? Is it because she treats others as she'd like to be treated and you don't give a hoot about their feelings? Is it because she makes friends and keeps them and you are constantly searching for new ones, wondering what happened to the old ones? Is it because she always makes a neat, clean appearance and yours is always in need of repair? Is it because she is liked for her honesty and your bragging and blowing-off is boring and uninteresting? Is it because she is proud of her race and the color of her skin, knowing that some will not want her friendship because of it, and you have doubts and fears about life, because yours is the color it is, and just because you're you?

Ask these questions of yourself, and if you answer them honestly, they will get you on the right track. Don't let your mistakes discourage you. Let them encourage you to do better. That is if you're big enough to know when you do wrong and smart enough to do something about it. This will boost your personality rating. If you're interested enough in you and your future, you'll do something about developing a pleasing and charming personality.

A NEW YOU

This cannot be done alone. You won't get to first base if you stay by yourself, without friends. You will never know what personality is all about. You will never understand yours. Friends can be important—more important to you, now, than ever before. They can help you make these changes. Let them tell you what kind of person you are. Don't pout and poke out your mouth when you hear things that don't satisfy you. You don't see yourself as others do. It's wonderful to know that a friend will love and respect you enough to be honest with you.

Some girls are known to be catty and jealous. Watch out for this kind. Who needs them? They are no good to themselves. All girls are not this way, so pick and choose your friends carefully. A real friend will want you to have a good personality and will help you. This kind is not easy to find.

Don't be a snob, but be particular about the choice of your friends. True friendship should mean much to you. Having a flock of friends is one thing, but keeping them is something else. This is why you must be particular in your selection. Your friends can make life more interesting and so much more fun. They will be a part of the things you do that you cannot do alone. They will make you think . . . not only about yourself but about others. They can furnish companionship and fill vacant places in your life with joy and happiness. They will provide support when it is needed. Most important, they will help you to be a stronger individual. This is essential in developing a more pleasing personality. A carefully selected group of friends help you develop poise . . . a necessity in this overcrowded world we live in. Well-balanced friendships are as necessary to you as the three well-balanced meals you eat each day. The kind of person you are is reflected in the company you keep.

Select those that you will be proud of. Those that you trust and those that you can depend on are worthwhile. A person's appearance or her popularity should not be yardsticks to measure friendship. Choose instead those friends who have quality . . . those you respect for just being the individuals they are. Your attitude toward others is clearly reflected by the number of friends you have. Who's got time for an unfriendly girl, or one with a chip on her shoulder or one who is quick to pick a fuss? When things go wrong, make sure you are not the one to start an argument. What a dreadful feeling when the others pair off and team up in groups and go on their merry way, leaving you on the sidelines. The world moves fast, and it's too bad, but there just isn't enough time to try to understand peculiar standoffish attitudes. It's so easy to be friendly, but you must do your share of the job. If you've been closed up in a shell or boxed in behind a stone wall, break out and live! True friends will make you feel at ease. They will learn to love you for your fine qualities. You must show them the same consideration.

SHARE YOUR FRIENDS

Be an agreeable friend. Naturally you will want to join in the fun, as long as it's good, clean, healthy fun. Once you break the ice and you feel good about the friends you have made, learn to be generous with them. Help them make new friends. Everybody has special friends. To these you feel very close and you have a special liking. So you want to keep them for yourself. But being possessive of your friends will only bring you unhappiness. Keep your feelings under control. Don't be mad when they go off to do things with others. Circumstances may make it possible to invite you each time. Be understanding! Share your friends. You will be happier for doing it and so will they.

ARE YOU SHY?

At your age, one of the greatest personality "hold backs" is shyness. Most girls (and boys too) are shy, at one time or another. A shy personality that is consistent can be a serious problem. But it can be corrected. Shyness is no big deal. It takes time to deal with yourself and others. Don't be afraid and don't be in a hurry. Shyness is fear.

This fear makes you nervous. What are some of the things that frighten you? Anything new . . . a new situation is generally the reason. A new school, new neighborhood, new job, meeting new people, even wearing new clothes are just a few reasons for you to be nervous and fall apart. Most times, you'd rather take a beating than to have to be with new people. If this is the case, put yourself in new groups more often. Don't wait to be introduced or wait for the other person to be the first to speak. The sooner you move in and do these things for yourself, the quicker the nervousness will disappear.

GET HOLD OF YOURSELF

If you go to a new school, it's frightening to face all those people you've never seen before. It won't be as bad if you know your appearance is right from head to toe. And just before you reach the school, take a deep breath, get control of your legs, hold your shoulders back and your head up with confidence, and walk right in, even if you pass a crowd on the way. Once you get past them, you'll feel much better. By the time you meet the principal or the new teacher, you'll be better able to carry on without difficulty.

You could almost die when you have to eat before strangers. If you know your manners are right, this shouldn't bother you too much. Don't be too hasty to get through the meal. Nerves will do this. You'll be a nervous wreck, not knowing what to do with the time, if you're the first one through. Take small helpings and eat slowly.

If talking adds to the nervousness . . . try listening. It's always better to let other people talk. Be especially interested when they talk about themselves. When you speak, "watch your mouth." Try to say the right thing. Some girls are guilty of "putting their big foot" right in their mouth, everytime they speak. It seems that you just can't say anything right. When this happens, it's hard to get yourself back together. Avoid this feeling, and think carefully before you speak. You can't always be right, but you can be most of the time. Work at your shy personality in small stages. You can't fight it all at one time. Correct step by step and in no time you'll find you're in control of your nerves and things don't bother you as much.

ADD BOYS TO THE LIST

Whatever your personality rating is, it's not a bad idea to balance out your friendships with a few boys added to the list. Almost every girl has at least one girl friend. But maybe what you need most is a boy friend or two. Not the kind you get real serious with. The boys that make real pals are the ones that might be more meaningful to you right now. The subject of boys included into your life cannot be overlooked. Boys add spark and happiness to the life of any girl. Believe it or not, boys are sometimes much more understanding than girls. It must be clearly understood that boys have personality just like girls. They too are shy and frightened at times. You must learn to deal with their habits, too.

All girls want to know more about boys, but some are scared of them. They think boys are "untouchable." It's kind of silly to go through life believing this. Boys make good friends. You can learn from boys . . . their likes and their dislikes, their activities and their behavior patterns. It's normal for boys to like you and you them. This will never happen if you're too shy to even say "hello." Every boy you know doesn't have to be your steady. You can be good friends without being "that way" about every boy you're seen with. One good thing, girls don't have to go far to meet boys. School is one of the best places I know. The library is another. A party is still better. Back in your mother's day, she had to wait for the boy to make the first move. But today, there's nothing wrong with your "breaking the ice" and being the first to say hello. He will be happy you did.

Girls with over-powering personalities frighten boys away. Boys have always liked girls who know how to act, those who are quiet and, when necessary, tender and feminine, even though boys may whistle and make wolf calls at the other kind. This will never change. When a boy wants to be serious, he looks for a girl with this kind of personality; one he can be with for a long time.

BUILD A FIRM FOUNDATION

Building a new personality is somewhat like building a house. The foundation must be firm enough to hold the kind of house you plan to build. One part must balance with the other. Your personality balance is poise. One is not much good without the other. All the things you do and say must balance . . . giving you self-confidence and self-assurance. Your footing must be sure, otherwise you will crumble just as a house will that doesn't have a strong foundation to hold it up. The inner you helps you to control the things you do and say.

Knowing what to say and when to say it is good, but if you have annoying mannerisms and gestures they can immediately put you on the spot. They give your weaknesses away every time. You don't want people whispering behind your back, "If she'd just stop fidgeting and fussing" . . . "What a lovely girl, but if she'd only stop pulling and tugging." Pulling on your ear, twisting and wringing your hands, playing with your necklace or the collar of your dress, twisting your handkerchief, pulling on your clothes, hanging onto the arm of your chair, swinging your legs, are just a few of the common gestures that express nervousness, tension and fright. Biting your fingernails or the side of your finger tips is one of the worse mannerisms and is the most common among girls. If you're guilty of this crime, it is the first bad habit you must try to overcome. Such mannerisms and gestures can spoil your appearance and destroy your charm.

Charm requires co-ordination of your mind and body and its movements. Know what to do and how to do it, and then do it as gracefully and femininely as you can. Your confidence and balance put you at ease in any situation, and add poise and personality to a charming and attractive you.

Remember pretty girls are not born that way. The prettiness of a girl comes from within. This prettiness must be developed. As you develop your personality, you develop a pretty you.

II

The Clothes You Wear

Your clothes spell out your personality . . . long before any of your other assets are seen.

Clothes make the woman, so they say. Don't you believe it! But they do help. They can make you look anyway you want to look. They can do wonders for you and your figure. The clothes you wear are one of the most important aspects of your personal appearance. Nothing perks you up and adds life to your personality as much as knowing you're well dressed for the occasion. Nothing destroys personality quicker than knowing you look all wrong with clothes that don't fit and are unbecoming. The amount of money you spend on your wardrobe is not the answer to being well dressed. It is you and your personality that can make a garment look expensive or cheap, depending on the way you wear it. The most expensive clothing in the world can look like two cents if it is not worn correctly, with the right accessories, or is incorrectly fitted . . . shortened or lengthened . . . and it is just not right for the person who is to wear it.

CLOTHES AND YOUR PERSONALITY

The clothes you wear don't always have to be brand new. You may be the younger member in the family and have to finish up wearing a garment started by an older sister or girl relative. This is not so hard to take. You just may be the girl who can do a lot for clothes . . . old or new . . . now that they belong to you. Your figure and your personality can give an old garment new life. In fact, you might look better in it than the original owner. On the other hand, you might be one of the girls who must always wear the clothes purchased for you by someone else . . . whether you like it or not. Quietly, you're protesting. But now you've reached the age of importance. Your interest in clothes has sprouted up from nowhere, and you like the feeling. It's going to be so much fun having some "say" about the clothes you wear. Your new interest in clothes will change your appearance. In no time, you'll have the "know how" to do things with your wardrobe. You will be able to come up with a dream of a wardrobe and it won't take a fat bankroll to do it. You can make a minimum wardrobe seem big and impressive with individuality, creativeness and good common sense. The basis for good grooming is intelligent planning and organization.

ORGANIZING — CLOSETS AND DRESSER DRAWERS

This organization must start in your clothes closet and in your dresser drawers. Closet habits can become clothing habits. The way you look betrays the state of your closet and bureau drawers. Your organization or disorganization leaves its mark on your appearance. The girl who has a place for her clothing and keeps everything neat and orderly is the girl who makes the best appearance . . . well-groomed and poised. But the girl who doesn't care about what happens to her clothes as she takes them off at the end of the day and is constantly having to look for things, makes a slovenly, sloppy, slipshod appearance. If this is you, you'd better get busy and straighten things up. Don't let your "at home" secrets give you away. Before new purchases are made, check over the things you already have, and check on the space available for your clothes.

Everyone has a problem with closets. The more things you have, the bigger your problem. If you live in an apartment in any overcrowded city, closet space is at a premium. No matter how much space you have, it still isn't enough. If your space is limited, try to keep it uncluttered. When clothes are put away properly, there is little chance they will need pressing before each wearing. Keep each piece where it belongs (in the closet or a box), fresh and clean to go at a moment's notice.

Rearrange your closet and dresser drawers often. You'll find that with each new organization job, you come up with a system that was better than the last. Easy-to-use contact paper is a good way to keep dresser drawers and clothes closets attractive and clean. Decorative shelf paper, if used with imagination, will help you do many "inside" tricks. Either one makes it possible to change colors and patterns as often as you tire of them.

If you dare to be different, save all the advertisement pages of the daily newspapers. Line the closet walls and floors with this mass of black and white print. Trim it with bright red scotch tape and red ribbon. When that begins to fade and looks dingy, strip the walls and start all over. This idea will only cost a few cents.

GETTING RID OF OLD CLOTHES

If your closet is jammed-packed with clothes and other things, weed them out. Get rid of the clothes you don't need and those you aren't wearing. If you've outgrown last year's clothing or find that is beyond repair, get rid of it, no matter how it hurts.

If there are no young members in your family to be made happy when you give clothes away, have swap sessions with your girl friends. Swap a too-tight sweater for a skirt that no longer fits her. This is fun and works effectively for both of you. Everybody profits from a swap session. It is much better to know that these items are being used rather than have them take up much-needed space in your closet or dresser drawers.

You are old enough now and you care about your appearance. It is your personal responsibility to see to it that the clothes you own are properly cared for . . . whether they number just one skirt and blouse or a closet jammed full. The value you get from the clothes you own, depends on the care and the value you put into them. For instance, you can get $55.00 worth of wear from a $5.00 skirt, if you take good care of it. On the other hand, a $55.00 skirt will not give you $5.00 worth of wear if it has been mistreated.

HANGERS, BOXES AND GARMENT BAGS

It's a lazy young miss who wastes her time making excuses. There are all sorts of gadgets for the closet that help you put your clothes away properly. A variety of hangers for dresses and suits are available. There are racks for skirts and hangers for blouses that hold six to eight pieces each, without wrinkling and crushing. Hat stands are good for the everyday beret or hat. There are colorfully printed or striped or the peep-hole cellophane boxes that beautifully preserve your "Sunday best" headgear. If you're smart and clever, you can make these yourself. With this care, your hats can go from season to season, looking just like new. Shoe racks keep your shoes off the floor where they collect dirt and dust.

Save the plastic bags that come from the neighborhood cleaners. They can be used over and over again as dust protectors. If your budget will allow it, choose garment bags with trimming to match a color scheme. They are especially handy for clothes that don't get daily use. Hang out-of-season clothing in garment (or paper) bags until you're ready to use them again. When putting clothes away, make sure all belts are hanging where they belong. Nothing is more upsetting than missing belts. If you like them all in one place, look for one of the large strong metal hooks; then you'll always know where they are.

SWEET SMELLING CLOSETS

Worn clothes with dirt and dust and body odors leave a musty odor in the closet. Keep your closet clean and sweet-smelling. If the closet needs it, try closet spray or sachet. Here is another good way to get every penny's worth from the bottle of your favorite cologne. Make it pay off right down to the last drop. Let that last drop add a clean sweetness to your clothes closet. Remove the cap and tuck the empty bottle into the corner of the closet or on the shelf. What a delightful fragrance your clothes will have! You will have an elegant feeling when you know your clothes are clean, and they smell that way. Try the same trick in the drawer space you occupy.

Clothes worn all day need airing before they go back into the closet. Body odors and food odors seep into the fabrics of your clothing. Unless these strong odors have time to disappear, they go back into the closet and spread ⁺his unpleasant odor into fresh clean clothing. Your closet sachet, cologne or clean-smelling closet spray doesn't have a chance. The shoes you wear also carry odors. If your feet perspire, the odor is that much stronger. When this happens, shoes need several hours of fresh air before they can be worn again or put away. Sitting out of the closet overnight is long enough for them to dry out completely. Leather shoes require polishing to keep them bright and sparkling. After each wearing, suede or fabric shoes must be dusted or brushed before they are put away. Do not allow the dust to settle. Carrying a small brush in your handbag will keep them free of dust and lint. A light brushing and wiping will help keep up their appearance and add to the life of the shoe.

BRUSHING, DUSTING, AIRING

Take some time, each month or so, to empty the closet completely. Everything looks better when it gets some air. Brushing, dusting and airing restores life to clothes that have been hanging without use. Spots and stains must be removed immediately. The longer they are neglected, the harder they are to get out. A light pressing (with a steam iron, if possible) removes wrinkles and keeps details and pleats sharp and neat. Your clothes should be kept spotlessly clean and ready for inspection on a moment's notice. If you can keep up this routine, this is real organization.

A STITCH IN TIME

As a last precaution, a stitch in time can save many a long rip and tear. Keep needle and thread handy. When a button begins to droop and hems sag, or threads begin to pop in seams and darts, put your needle and thread to work. It's maddening when dressing to find hooks and snaps missing. lace ripping and seams popping. No matter how minor the repair, do it promptly.

MAKING NEW PURCHASES

If you're now faced with the responsibility of making your own purchases, there are some things you should know before you buy one stitch.

Be well informed about current fashions. Read your fashion magazines and look closely at all the things you would like to own, whether you ever do or not. When you see something you like in a newspaper or magazine, cut it out. Study each item as if it were yours. Copy some of the ideas you see when you go window shopping. You can wear a fifty-cent scarf the same way a five dollar one is displayed in one of the windows of your favorite retail stores.

One of the really important things to know about the clothes you want to own is the fabric. This is important whether you can make your own clothes from a pattern, or buy them ready-made for you. If you know how to sew and make some of the clothes in your wardrobe, it will be easy for you to learn about the fabrics and how to care for them from the salespeople in the fabric departments of the neighborhood stores. There are hundreds of new fabrics on the market; each with a combination of fiber content. You must know how to care for each, so the garment can be worn for a long time.

THE PERSONALITY OF FABRICS

Many of these new fabrics can be washed . . . by hand or in the washing machine. They require little or no ironing. Garment manufacturers have made it easy for you, when you buy clothes ready-made. There is a tag attached to everything you buy today. This tag is important and valuable. If you read it, you will get long service from your clothes. It will tell you everything you need to know about its care. Read and follow the instructions carefully. Then you're bound to get your money's worth from every piece of clothing you buy. There is no reason why you should not look your best at all times.

For those garments that are washable, there are now soaps on the grocery shelf that get your clothes clean in cold water. This is protection for all new fabrics. Fabrics need cleaning protection as well as protection from body odors. Some new fibers carry their own strange odors, and need additional help to keep them unnoticed.

Familiarize yourself with the washing products that are best for your sweaters and the ones that wash your cottons effectively without damage to colors or shrinkage. Know those washing products that keep your nylon pretties free of tattletale-gray. Protect the life of your clothes and select the all-purpose soap or detergent that will have a long-wearing, durable effect on the fabric content of each garment.

Any garment that will not fare well in the washtub must have special care. If some of your clothing demands dry cleaning, make sure it gets this kind of treatment . . . with caution! Don't be in a great hurry to take things to the cleaners. Too many dry cleanings will wear your clothes out before they've had an opportunity to give a proper performance. When cleaning is beyond your personal touch, that is the time for professional mechanical cleaning—and not before. It is a bad habit, every time a spot is visible, to rush your clothes out to the dry cleaners.

Fabrics play games. They can make you look larger or smaller, depending on the thickness. They can help you hide figure faults or add to figure flattery. Heavy thick fabric is sure to add inches to the figure. Fabric that is sheer and clingy reveals all your figure secrets. The design or pattern of the fabric can make you look taller or shorter, depending on the way the lines go. If the pattern moves up and down in vertical fashion, you will look taller. Moving from side to side in horizontal fasion, your body will look shorter and wider.

UNDERARM PROTECTION

Wearing underarm shields during the winter months when you wear heavy woolen clothing, especially those that require dry cleaning, protects them from underarm and body odors. Woolen fabrics hold odors longer than lighter-weight and sheer ones do. Underarm shields are required to keep down unpleasant odors, otherwise the moisture penetrates and even the dry cleaning can't remove these deep-set odors.

Try those shields that either pin or tack into the sleeves or those with shoulder and arm bands. The newest ones stay securely in place with a band that fits under the bosom and hooks in back. Another new style works the same way, but with sheer net bosom cups that hold your breasts easily and comfortably, just as a brassiere would do. The style you select must be one that is comfortable to wear and easy to care for. They must be washed out after each wearing. The style that sews in is fine for dresses that don't get frequent wearings. If this type is used the shields must be completely dry before the garment is hung away in the closet.

CLEAN FROM THE SKIN OUT

Every fashion-loving female must be clean from skin out. Girls who are careful about their outer appearance want the cleanest clothes next to their skin. You are nowhere and the fashion battle is only half won if you are caught with dirty underclothes. They deserve the same careful attention you give those worn on the outside. Don't think for one minute you can slip by, just one time, with dirty, dingy underwear going unnoticed. That's always the time you're sure to get caught. Nothing can spoil your appearance more than a dirty slip edge peeping out from the hemline of a clean, well cared for skirt.

The closest thing next to your skin might just be a pair of panties, or panty hose, panty girdle or garter belt. These foundation garments, known as your secret partners in fashion, require little attention, but they demand to be kept clean. These little help-mates are great assistants in smoothing out bumps and bulges that break the sleek line of your outer clothing. Time was when girls your age wouldn't think of such things—when there were no such garments available for young still-developing figures. But today the control story is different. You are just the right age to get acquainted with these undergarments that help you keep your good figure.

UNDERGARMENT CONTROL

For the present you may need only a comfortable easy-to-wear bra and soft panty girdle that smooths you out in the right places. At your age, you should not be heavily caged in bones and stiff elastic. If your figure is such that it needs additional firming, there are garments that are youthfully constructed with feather-light boning or a power net reinforced front and back panel that will give you sufficient support. These garments are comfortable to wear, leaving your body firm and smooth with freedom of body motion . . . a big help to you and your figure problems. Check the department store in your favorite shopping area that has full stock on undergarments for girls in your age group. Discuss your figure problems with the salespeople in charge. They have had training to advise and suggest garments that will ease your figure worries. Any hidden garment must get the best care. Read and follow the washing instructions carefully.

When you start out in the morning, check every piece of clothing, and make sure they are clean enough to pass a "spic and span" examination. Sheer nylons and drip-dry fabrics make it possible for underclothes to be laundered at night and dry before you get up the next morning. Start the habit, now, of doing some laundry work each night as you prepare for bed, even if you have a dozen changes. This good habit takes so little time, and every stitch is always clean. There is no in-between mark to cleanliness. Be clean, all the way, from skin out!

This is the kind of girl that boys want to meet and be with. It's this kind of girl who stands out in the crowd. If this is the picture of you, then you're one whom your friends will be proud of. What pleasure you'll get out of receiving compliments from boys on your appearance. You'll get a greater pleasure when the girls break down and tell you how nice you look. It may take them a long time to get around to it, but when they do, they usually mean it.

BUILDING A WARDROBE

When you're ready to go out on a shopping spree, don't spend a penny on one stitch until you know all there is to know about your figure type. The kind of life you live and where will help you decide on the kind of clothes you must have. You know what you have on hand, and now you know what you must have to make the well-balanced wardrobe.

A wise shopper is one that takes her time, learning as she moves along to develop good taste, choosing clothes that look well on her. Avoid panic buying. Don't be one of those girls that must buy something every time they get their little hot hands on a dollar. Panic shopping always leads to fashion failure. When you buy in a hurry, you only think you like what you've bought. Later on, you discover it wasn't for you in the first place.

Take a good look (in a long mirror) at your figure. Recheck your personality. Even though you may make some changes, work with it as it is today. Let the clothing changes come with the changes in your personality. Your figure may fit into the petite, junior petite, teen, sub-teen, junior or misses size. Your age doesn't matter. Your height and the size of your body tells you in which group your figure belongs. All these different sizes are found in the popular department stores. Pattern companies have pattern designs in each one of these sizes. Either way you decide to shape up a good fashion wardrobe, you can have a perfect fit. Once you've given your size and shape careful consideration, then and only then can you start with a wardrobe plan to fit.

WHAT ARE YOU REALLY LIKE

If you're short, thin and delicate, you must be a "petite." If so, you look for clothes that help you keep this dainty feminine look. Easy-moving lightweight fabrics, ruffles, lace, ribbons and soft dainty touches should do the trick. Heavy, bulky fabrics, bold plaids and prints will be overpowering to your small frame. Straight, slim silhouettes will add height if they are not body-hugging and sexy looking.

With a figure that seems to be going "out" instead of "up" you probably fit into the sub-teen sizing. Let's hope this figure is only temporary. But until the time you've slimmed your figure down, you will want clothes that will make you look long and lean and not wider and broader. You will, naturally, avoid big checks and blocked plaids that will make you look shorter and wider, attracting attention. Straight, up-and-down stripes and lines will minimize the width and add to your height. Clothes that are well co-ordinated but not attention-getters are what you should aim for.

A ROUND FIGURE

A full figure . . . one that is not wide and fat, but heavier in spots than you're happy with can be quickly trimmed down first, by wearing a foundation garment that will hold some of the "bigness" in place. You should never give a second glance at a dress to make you look bigger, let alone wear one. Bright-colored, garish costumes must be pushed aside, for the time being . . . at least until you've lost some of the extra inches and pounds. Too much of any one thing only adds to the bulk already there. Medium to dark basic colors will slim down the figure. In warmer climates, for a figure that is "larger than it should be," try cool slimming tones of soft blues, beiges and greens with straight casual lines.

LEAN AND LANKY

You're lucky if you're the willowy, tall, fashion model type. You never had it so good! You can wear almost everything you see in the fashion magazines. New fashion silhouettes will find themselves right at home on your body. Your height gives you the privilege of carrying any color or boldness of pattern with ease and elegance. Because of your height, you may have to ease up on the stress you place on "pencil straight lines," which will naturally make you look taller. Belts worn at any point—above or below the natural waistline—take away some of the height. Bulky tweeds and woolens, bold stripes and strong details make you outstanding and attractive. Your skirts can be shorter than most, and you can take color and fashion combinations that other figures cannot.

FIND YOUR SIZE

You may fit any one of these figure categories. That's for you to decide. If you're not sure, try for size when you go shopping. Have someone take your measurements. Jot them down and keep them with you when you go out to buy. The length of your waist from the back of your neck to the waistline is an important measurement to have, and especially if you're buying a pattern.

Whatever grouping your figure falls into, there are certain basic items that belong in almost every wardrobe. A wardrobe built around substantial basics guarantees you a successful fashion future. Every wise shopper works with a budget. If you really want to stretch yours, learn to sew. The budget that would ordinarily take you through one season might make it through two if you make some of your own clothes. This is not to mention how individual you can be, having just the right lines and details that almost play magic with your figure. Even if you're not good enough in dressmaking, knowing how to make minor adjustments will help. It costs money every time a skirt has to be shortened, a seam taken in, a zipper moved or a neckline raised.

BALANCE YOUR WARDROBE BUDGET

Juggle your budget so you can spend a little more money on one good dress, suit or coat, cut on plain, undefined lines. The possibilities for various accessories are unlimited. Your clothes look different with each accessory change. Every girl should own at least one suit. A clever girl shops for one that can be worn with separate blouses and a change in sweaters. If your figure can take it, a suit with a contrasting jacket is good. If the budget will not allow for contrasting colors, stick with one that is basic in fabric, line and color. It's good if the skirt can be worn by itself with other tops. Then the jacket can be worn with other skirts, slacks or shorts. Build several outfits from one suit. If you live out of the city and spend much of your time outdoors, put a lot of time and thought in your suit purchase. You need one that will do many more things for you and the way you live. Pants suits, walking suits with divided skirts or three piece suits that can be mixed up with your own combinations, will add mileage to your wardrobe. It will be so much more fun seeing just how far you can go with separate purchases.

DOLLARS AND SENSE IN COAT PURCHASES

Putting a few more dollars into one good coat . . . one that will take you many places . . . is smarter than having two that cost less. A coat is one of the most important items in your wardrobe. It should last for several seasons. It will if it's of good top quality. A bright pretty color is one that you will tire of, and will "announce" your appearance every time you wear it. If it's your one and only good coat, it must be a color that goes well with almost any other color in your present wardrobe. If you can own more than one, that's fine. You can be more daring with color.

Consider your wardrobe and shop wisely. Don't settle on the first coat you see. If you're mad for fur, you're best off if the fur trim is removable. If the fur is not the "real McCoy" it may not last for two seasons. All your friends will think you have a new coat when you show up in the same coat next season . . . without the fur trim. You may prefer a walking-length or jacket-type coat for school, but your "one and only" coat may have to be worn to school on days when the weather demands it. It must also cover you on dates and for dress-up and special occasions. Since you're putting a few more dollars into this purchase, you must buy one that fits you and the winter season where you live. It must be right in every way and must be equipped to give you winter-long protection.

DON'T IGNORE FASHION

Style trends come and go, but basic good design goes on forever. Fashion trends are important and a careful study must be made of new fashion looks and silhouettes before new clothes are bought. Naturally, you will want to buy clothes that are new-looking. But the wise young shopper is one who looks for fashion trends that have durability. Those that have a welcomed "stay put" appearance are the ones that will be your best investment. Trend-setting styles may bloom out like balloons or may hug your body like wallpaper with hemlines way above the knees. Don't be such a slave to fashion that you must have it anyway. Don't be roped in by any fashion look unless it's right on you. Many new fashion silhouettes that hit the popularity jack pot are the ones that fade out the fastest. Avoid fashion fads. You and your figure must get first-grade consideration. This is your investment for the future.

Balancing a wardrobe can be tricky, unless you assess yourself and your way of life. It would be kind of silly to own a lot of party dresses and never go to parties. It would be just as "wild" to have a wardrobe full of pants when your life calls for dresses. There is no sense to having too many of one item and not enough of another. After the basic costumes are bought, look for separate items. They are the best wardrobe builders. Separate sweaters, skirts, jackets and blouses are the most wonderful things that have happened to fashion for many a century. Whether you're in school or out, you will want as many separates in your wardrobe as your budget will allow. With fashion intelligence you will have enough clothing to carry you through many seasons. These clothing pieces can build countless costumes, even if you're limited to just two of each kind. Knowing the possibilities of each is what will make you well dressed.

FOUR SEASONS

If you live where the year is broken into definite seasons, your shopping must be planned accordingly. For summer, you will want as many changes as possible. Cottons are cool and comfortable, especially those of drip-dry fabrics that require no ironing. Just one skirt with several blouses can take you through the entire summer season.

At other times of the year, again, you want the assurance of always looking your best. You will have this if every item is put to work to make you look the part each time you go out. "Hot" fashion items hit the stores like wildfire. They are seen every time you look around. What everybody else is wearing just might be the one look you will want to stay away from. There's nothing smarter than individuality in dressing. Be independent, stand on your own two feet, make fashion decisions for yourself. If you're a girl with a flair for clothes you can get away with many things. Learn to be your own critic. Look at the clothes you wear and the way you wear them with an unbiased eye.

WHERE DO YOUR SKIRTS STOP?

One of the main topics for fashion discussion is "where do your skirts stop?" Where your hemline stops is really your own business, just as long as you know it's stopping at the attractive point on you. If your legs are more straight than shapely, an attractive stopping point may not agree with what fashion dictates. Don't worry about it! Make decisions that are best for you. Remember the thigh-high skirts? Even the girls that did not decide to let their skirts go that high were not fashion castoffs. You

won't be either if your decision goes in the opposite
direction.

CHOOSING COLORS

Color, color and more color is the cry on the fashion
scene. You read and hear a great deal about color choices
suitable for complexions of other races, but seldom is
anything said about the right colors for members of dark
races. The color range of our skin tones is so large and
varied, a definite pattern of color choices would be difficult to follow. Every complexion, from the lightest to the
darkest, has very prominent undertones. One thing is
sure, most dark complexions should keep away from
bright glaring colors, but some, depending on the under-
tone of the skin, do take bright colors effectively. This is a
problem that must be worked out individually. If you
hold a color to your face, your common sense will tell you
whether it is good for you or not. Follow fashionable color
trends if those colors are complimentary to your skin
tone.

A hit-and-miss color program in your wardrobe can get
you into serious trouble. Colors that are good mixers are
those to shoot for. New colors are extremely important,
in that they are shocking, extremely bright and gay.
Many of these strong bright colors can be worn as attractively by "colored" skins as those with white, pale skin—
often much better. These new colors can be worn in one
color sweep or interestingly combined depending on the
color of the skin. Very often bright colors make the un-
dertone of the skin more attractive and the face more
noticeable. Colors must be appealing to you . . . your
skin . . . your eyes . . . your hair . . . and to your
figure. Sticking with dark, drab, lifeless colors is one of
the worst fashion mistakes brown skin girls make. If you
are the type who can be daring, bring the brights up next
to your face. Bright, strong, vibrant colors bring out fa-

cial beauty even to the darkest skins. If you've been afraid, try it. You'll be glad you did.

If it makes you feel better, start with colors first. Pick those that are best for you, then build your wardrobe around them. With this technique you will always look as if you're wearing something different. The right colors, properly selected, can change your mood and put pep into your costume. The touch of a crisp white color or a bright scarf gives added life to dark clothes, although the dark clothes minimize the size of the figure. Dark skins look much better if a touch of color is added to dark basic tones, breaking the line between the face and body.

FASHION ACCENTS OR ACCENT ON ACCESSORIES

Place a strong accent on your accessories. These are the little extras that add big importance to your grooming. These additions can solve many dressing problems, but there's a secret to using them. They can either make or mar your appearance. That little addition can make the outfit look better if it isn't overdone. That's the secret . . . knowing when to stop.

A little thing like a scarf can be the most important item in your accessory department. You can do hundreds of things with just a simple square or length of silk. Did you ever try tying it to the handle of your umbrella on a cloudy or rainy day? Or you can tie one fashionably and attractively on your head when the weather is bad, or for a ride in an open car, or a long walk on a cold, crisp day or maybe wear a matching one to your swim suit or pool-side printed shift.

Scarfs are all right in their right places. But as you grow older your need for hats will grow depending on your type of life. Get into the habit of wearing hats. Hats help you look more lady-like and provide a finished appearance to your "special" costumes. Select one that doesn't muss your hairdo, one that goes with most things in your wardrobe.

A girl just can't get along without little accessories such as a pair of white fabric (or leather) gloves, and a single strand of pearls (fake or real). White gloves go well with all your costumes. Fabric gloves are easy to care for and will last for many seasons with careful treatment. The leather ones will look better and last longer when they are cleaned professionally. You may be one to take jewelry or leave it alone. You may never own more than a single strand of pearls and matching button earrings. They are necessary to every young girl's accessory box. They will go with anything and will assure you of a neat well-groomed appearance. If your money holds out and you like jewelry, a collection of fashionable fake jewelry can be valuable to you and your dressing habits. Jewelry must be used with caution. Too much on a young girl makes her look tacky and junky. It's always smart to be without it rather than have it spoil the fashion image you're trying to create.

SCHOOL CLOTHES

Most girls your age are in school . . . full or part-time (working for that diploma demands it of you). Your school clothes should be simple and neat.

Easy-to-get-into sweaters, blouses and skirts are a necessity unless your school requires you to wear a uniform. Comfort and simplicity are classroom requirements. Pleated, slim or full skirts usually walk away with high fashion honors. Avoid complicated fashions. Buy simple one-piece dresses that look good with a sweater or your school jacket.

If your school is one of the few that allow pants on the campus, in many ways you're lucky. It will cut down on other purchases, if you have the figure for pants. If you do, selecting a top to go with them will be no problem.

There are plenty to choose from, and many slacks and shorts come with their own matching top. Pants go many more places today. Where you live may have certain restrictions. It's great to be different and have all eyes turn to stare, if these are admiring glances. But just to create excitement is no joke. Wear pants only where you know they will be accepted.

If school is the place where you're spending most of your time and doing most of your walking, then comfortable shoes must be on your shopping list. The plain loafer-type are popular. So are boots. But boots are not to be worn all day long in a hot classroom. They could be just the fashion touch your short, short skirt needs, but indoors they are uncomfortable and do unneccessary harm to your feet. Supply yourself with enough socks to carry you through at least one week, with everyday changes (this is protection against dampness). Ankle and knee-length socks in colors that go with your outfits are a campus must.

Big carry-all handbags are popular and very handy to hold all your school equipment. Make sure they are orderly and neat and things are in their right place.

A girl with a "A" rating in school or out is one who selects a school wardrobe that can be used at other times. With a change of accessories, any of your school clothes should carry you elsewhere comfortably and correctly.

DRESS-UP CLOTHES

If you're a lucky girl who has many dates, the clothes you wear do not have to have a "special" tag hanging on them. Naturally, you want more than anything to look well to the man in your life . . . and if the date is an informal or casual one, some of the separates you wear to school will come in mighty handy. Your good suit will take you lots of places and you'll have that "just right" look. A jumper worn with or without a blouse is another

good standby for dating. It can even be last year's . . .
with clever accessories he will never know. There is no
end to the number of outfits you have in two-for-the-
price-of-one costume . . . a dress with a matching or
contrasting jacket.

GOING ON A DATE

Since most girls "go out of their minds" over a date, how
much serious thought do you give to dressing for yours?
Girls your age often place too much stress on casual
dressing for dates and parties. For week-end swing sessions, sure, you're more comfortable in a sweater and
skirt or easy moving shift dress or suit. You get into the
habit of checking with the other kids. If you don't wear
what the others do, you feel like an outcast. Why not
make your own decisions, and just for the heck of it,
make a dress-up party. You own one dress that moves
and swings just as easily as that skirt. It's true and sometimes heart-breaking if the boy you're dating dresses one
way, you must go along with it (if you want to go out
with him), even if it doesn't please you. It's a real "gas"
when you dream of getting into your "Sundaybest" and
here comes your date in sneakers and jeans. If you've had
it, getting disappointed in this situation, why not drop the
hint and say "let's get dressed up Friday night. You wear
your collar and tie and I'll wear my new green dress." Any
jerk should get that message. That special feeling of
being with that "dream of a man" just isn't the same if
you wear a skirt and shirt every time you go to the
movies.

BE YOUR PRETTIEST AT A PARTY

If it's a prom, naturally you'll want to wear your prettiest
party dress, and you will expect your date to be dressed

appropriately. Even if you go to a picnic or beach party, two people look good together only if they're dressed for the occasion. This is the thrill of owning clothes. They make you think. Making clothing changes, although they may be limited, makes your life a little more exciting and interesting.

LOOKING FOR A JOB

If you're not doing some work . . . after school or on Saturdays . . . you soon will. You may be looking for work, now. If so, it is important for you to make a good impression when you go to apply for a job. The clothes you wear must be neat and attractive. The sloppy sweaters and jackets you wear to school are taboo. Wear a simple dress, suit, or one of your nicest sweaters and skirts. Select what you want to wear in a conservative color. Avoid bright glaring shades. Make sure all wrinkles and creases have been removed, collar and cuffs are fresh and clean, and powder stains have been removed from your neckline.

Wear your simple jewelry, but nothing that makes a noise. Shoes must be polished or brushed, stocking seams straight and no runs. Wearing a hat is optional. Your gloves will help your appearance. Make sure your face is scrubbed clean, with light natural makeup application, your hands are clean and your fingernails have a well-cared-for look. An attractive appearance will help you get the job. A slipshod sloppy appearance will spoil your chances. If you're prepared, your chances are just as good as those of the other fellow, even though his face might be another color.

Once you get the job, the same rules can be applied to the clothes you wear in the office. The good impression you made during the interview must continue while you hold down the job. It has been said, in business circles, that blacks in business dress more attractively than the others. This may be because the spotlight is always on the dark face on the job. So, whatever you do on your job, be dressed appropriately. Looking neat and attractive is the requisite for any job, in an office, factory, or behind closed doors of a stock room. If you're on a job for the first time, whether it's full time, part time or just a little time after school, your appearance will help you keep it and just may be the reason for getting one better.

Dress simply and conservatively. Plunging necklines and sun-back dresses have never been accepted in business. Socks are fine for school but not for business (unless you've been told it is acceptable). If you have an after-school job, it's to your advantage to change to your stockings before you report for duty.

You can avoid a hurried, harried look if you plan in advance what you want to wear. Wherever you go, your clothes will speak for you. Visualize how you want to look and make that your goal, as long as your fashion picture is realistic. When you feel confident that you've done your best and you look right for the occasion, you will always make your best appearance.

12

The Way You Act

If you don't know how to act, owning all the pretty clothes in the world won't help you one single bit. The way you wear your hair, the way you fix your face, the beauty of your body and all your other assets can be quickly destroyed if your actions don't add up to those of a lady. A real beauty . . . inside and out . . . must first act like one.

Boys really go for girls who know what to do and when to do it . . . what to say and when it should be said. One of their chief complaints is, "Girls are silly, they don't know how to act." Boys won't tell you when your actions are not what they should be. You just don't see them again. The way you act can make a boy comfortable or uncomfortable. If you know this, why not do something about it? You may as well face up to it—it is the boys you want to please. Boys are choosey. The toughest boy in the neighborhood wants a girl he can be proud of. He wants a girl who not only knows how to dress, but one whose actions add up to the way she looks in her clothes.

Since it's the boys you're anxious to please, just for the heck of it let's run down a short list of things that boys don't like about girls. I've checked with a small group of boys in New York City and here are some of their pet peeves. They all said before a date they hate to sit around waiting for a girl, even if they do know her parents. They want to get going. It makes them nervous to have to have long conversations with adult members of the family. Some say it's even worse, when she finally shows and makes a mad dash back to the bedroom for a forgotten article and takes another hour to reappear. Another boy said it really burns him up when he takes a girl out to eat and she tries to order everything on the menu, and complains of being full only when she's half-finished with the food she ordered. Most boys don't like girls to wear heavy makeup. Others dislike girls that don't wear any. The entire group said they could "just die" when a girl dresses so that he is ashamed of a too-short skirt or a too-low neckline. They also dislike girls that accompany them to proms with furs and jewelry that make them look too grown-up. With all the smoking that goes on today, it's surprising that boys don't like a girl who smokes "like it's going out of style," just because she thinks this is necessary to be a member of the group. They just hate girls that are dirty and more than that . . . girls that talk loud, and especially in public. One boy strongly stated that he dislikes girls who double date and talk only to their girl friends all during the date. This same young man just can't take a girl that is always correcting him, who uses big words and always tells him what they mean. The boys all strongly agreed that they can do without a girl that is always "making up" to their best friend. One of the quiet boys said he dislikes a girl that never has her own money, and asks him for money for the ladies' room or ten cents to make a phone call. One of the last complaints is the dislike for girls who join in on the dirty jokes that boys tell and even have one better. On the other hand, they all said, even the quiet boy, that they are very uncomfortable with a girl who is too quiet and shy. They like a girl that knows her way around, and knows how to act as she moves. This is just half of all the things they told me, but it would take too long to go through the entire list of complaints. You can take it from here. They said it, I didn't!

FOLLOW THE RULES

The rules of good manners and everyday living are not as hard to follow as they seem. The basic day-to-day rules seldom change. If you follow these never-changing ones, your common sense will get you through other situations. Minding your manners, no matter where you are and whom you're with, will make it possible for you to go anywhere in ease and comfort. Knowing how to act can get you anywhere, accepted and comfortable.

If you're one of the lucky ones, your basic rules for good behavior were first learned and practiced at home. It was here where you learned the simple courtesies— thank you . . . please . . . excuse me . . . I'm sorry, etc. At the baby stage, you were taught to say and do the right thing. This is where it all started and it should have continued from there. The way you act in your own home will help things run more smoothly when you're away from home. Your actions at school, at church, at work, on the street and in public places, will indicate whether you've had good "at home" training.

If you didn't pay attention to this early instruction, blame only yourself. This is the training that gave you your start in life. If you decided somewhere along the way to make your own rules and do things as you pleased, it is still not too late to alter your behavior. This is a good time to make bad manners good. It is never too late to learn the rules of good manners . . . and home is as good a place as any. When things are done correctly there, you won't make mistakes when you're elsewhere.

Good manners only mean the consideration you show for others. Being kind to other people should not be too difficult. This kindness makes the world a better place to live. We all want that but we can't have it unless we can get along with the people we live and come in contact with as we move about.

PRACTICE AT HOME

Home is what you make it! Good manners will help make it a better place to be. Starting the day off with a cheerful greeting to those who live under the same roof helps one to be happy when people are greeted on the outside. What better way is there to start the day? When you begin this way, things run smoothly for the rest of the day. Your family, whether there are one or ten, should be very dear to you. Why not let them know it by your actions?

INTRODUCTIONS

Home is the place where you can practice all the rules of etiquette and good manners . . . like introductions. Know how you fumble when you're faced with introducing? It's neglectful (and disrespectful) to have your friends streaming in and out of the house without introducing them to your parents. Here is a good way to get some practice. Then when you're faced with introductions, you can follow through without a flaw. If introductions make you feel shaky, you need more practice. This will soon help you overcome your panic. "Mother, I would like you to meet my friend, Jessie Smith," is the way you introduce your friend to your mother. If you are ever in doubt, remember to use the adult name first. When introducing a boy and girl, say the girl's name first. This rule holds till you're fully grown. The female's name is called first. Accepting introductions can be just as easy. For the very young, simply say "hello." For older people "how do you do" is all that is required.

At home, you must learn how to act with other older people. When friends of your parents arrive, you wouldn't think of remaining in your seat. You are on your feet immediately. "Mrs. Jones, this is my daughter, Mary Lou," you hear your mother say. A polite "How do you do, Mrs. Jones," is all that is expected of you. Unless other questions follow, you quietly leave the room if you are not included in the conversation. Anyone visiting in your home should be treated the way you'd like to be treated if you were visiting them. If your favorite TV program is interrupted because of visiting guests, even if it kills you inside, accept it gracefully, and especially if they are friends of your parents. A hateful attitude will only lead to a big family "blow up" later on. Avoid as much unpleasantness as you can. Keep your home happy. Good manners will help!

TABLE MANNERS

Bad manners are apt to show up at the table more than any place else. If you think you can get away with bad table manners, at home, you'll surely slip up when you're eating somewhere else. Improving table manners at home relieves the strain of uncertainty when an out-to-dinner invitation comes along. Even if you're eating with a large group, bad manners have a way of appearing at a time when everyone is looking. If you're in the habit of sitting down with your family to a meal, with the table set properly, when you're out you will know how to eat and what to eat with. Many people get upset when they see more than a knife, fork, and spoon at their place setting. Don't let silverware frighten your appetite away.

Working parents often don't have the time to set a table with all the fixings. In this case, it's up to you to learn what to do and do it correctly. It's nice if you can sit down to a family meal. This is the time of day when you are all together. But you may not be this lucky. Irregular working hours of members of your family may mean that you must eat alone. This is no reason for you to eat without good manners. Neither does it mean that you should skip or miss meals. Eating alone is not so bad, it's just getting used to the idea. Even eating alone can be done with good table manners. They make eating a pleasure, not only for you, but those who eat with you.

With your plate taking the center spot, the fork goes to the left and the knife to the right. If spoons are necessary for your meal, they go to the right side of your knife. When placing silverware on the table, you will never go wrong if you place it in the order that it is to be used. For if salad forks are included with the family silver, by all means place it on the inside of the regular fork, when salad is being served. Otherwise it is all right to eat with your regular fork.

USE A NAPKIN

A napkin is a must when you sit down to a meal. The cloth one is not always necessary. Paper napkins are serviceable and popular. They are colorful and pretty, and some look and feel like cloth. If you are left to eat alone, and neither are available, use a paper towel. Fold it and place it where your napkin should be . . . to the left of your plate. Your water glass sits right in line with your knife. If you're drinking milk or any other beverage, that glass goes where the water glass is placed, unless you have both on the table at the same time. If so, the other glass is placed a little to the outside of the water glass and at an angle above it. It's nice if you can put your bread and butter on a plate all to itself. If you do so, that small plate goes on the left side, a little above the tip of your fork.

NEVER — NEVER — NEVER

Whether you're eating at home or somewhere else here are some NEVER rules for you to watch for. Never talk with your mouth full of food. Never have both hands working at the same time, unless you are cutting meat, salad, or buttering your bread. Never eat french fried potatoes (all right for crisp shoe string ones), asparagus, gooey pies and cakes with your fingers or any other foods that can't be eaten without dripping and running. Never wave silverware in the air while you're eating. Never eat with both elbows on the table (you may rest one there between courses). Never blow on your food. Let it stand until you can eat it comfortably. Never stretch and reach across the table for food on the other side. Have it passed to you. Never wad or crumble your napkin. Once you have used it, fold it loosely and place it to the left side of your plate. Never, never suck your teeth. Never dig for food left between your teeth with a toothpick. True the toothpick is for removing particles of food, but gouging and digging as you sit at the table is ugly and something a lady (or man, for that matter) should not do. The toothpick is also an ugly sight left in the corner of the mouth. Once you have used it, discard it.

Never interrupt the meal of the person sitting next to you by reaching in front of him, even if you do it with an "excuse me." Never crumble bread or crackers into your soup bowl. Never dive into the food as if you're starving to death. Wait for the others, no matter how it hurts. Never dip and dunk. (If you must, do it at home, when nobody, but nobody, is looking.) Never suck spaghetti into your mouth as it dangles in mid-air from your fork.

Learn to wrap it around your fork or break it in small pieces so it can be eaten with no mess. Never leave your spoon in a cup or glass while you drink from it. Never leave it in a glass or cup when you're through stirring. Never use your fingers as a pusher.

Never butter bread or rolls all at one time. Break off a piece and butter as you go along. Never drink from your saucer or your soup bowl. Never use your silverware to serve yourself—every serving dish should have its individual serving spoon or fork. Your silverware should stay at your eating place for your use only. Never taste food and put it back on the serving plate. Once it goes to your mouth, you're stuck with it. Never place your personal belongings on the table, during a meal (hat, handbag, gloves, etc.). Never apply make-up at the table, especially if you're dining out with the opposite sex. He is not interested in your makeup secrets. This certainly does not complete the "never do" list, but these few don'ts should keep you out of trouble while dining, at home or away.

ENTERTAINING YOUR FRIENDS

Learn how to entertain at home. Have your friends in often. That is, with permission from the family. It's good to know how to be a hostess, whether it's entertaining your date or a house full. Plan and prepare the meal yourself. Successful parties can be given with very little money spent. Stay within your budget and have fun . . . you can do it. Start your party off by being prepared and ready for your guests beforehand, even if it's just a couple of girl friends who have been invited to listen to your latest records. It's inconsiderate to keep invited guests waiting until you've finished your dressing. You'll make a big hit with the boys if you are ready on time. Boys hate to wait for girls. It's not cute to have that I-don't-want-him-to-think-I'm-sitting-around-waiting-for-him feeling.

FOLLOW FAMILY RULES

If you're entertaining a large group, discuss the plans with your parents. It's your party and your friends, but your parents must be satisfied with the party plans. Don't be discouraged if they don't agree with all you want. When it's over and done with, you'll see that everybody had just as much fun as if you had had your whole way. "Spiked punch" or alcoholic drinks are usually the topic for discussion in party planning. If drinking is permitted at your parties, this permit must come from the head of the family. Parents aren't square if they don't go for all the action you want at a party. If they say "no" with good reason . . . go along with it. It's their home too. Respect them and it!

Whatever the family rules are, you must abide by them. Your parents may feel that it's much better to have a little "spirit" at home than have you seek it elsewhere. If they are that considerate make sure you and your guests can take it. Watch your step! One of the biggest mistakes girls make today is drinking. Too many think they must drink to attract the attention of the boys. They'd much rather you didn't touch the stuff at all; you're prettier that way.

It's fine if you watch your P's and Q's when you're at home, but letting your hair down when you're away from the watchful eyes of your parents is all wrong. You need not be a "goody-goody," but don't be a "follow the leader." Don't let the others tempt you. Don't be easily lead astray from what you know is right. If your girl friends drink and the sight of the stuff makes you sick, leave it alone. If you know you can't take it, then it's not for you. But if you allow yourself to be dared into drinking more than you can hold gracefully, you're the one who pays in the end. Even punch with a "kick" in it, if overdone, can leave its aftereffects. Drinking is a dangerous and serious problem. Many dangers lie ahead when one is under the influence of alcohol. If you can stand on your own two feet and refuse things that you know are not good for you, you'll be liked better for it, in the long run.

Parties can be just as much fun without alcohol. If you're not of age to be thinking of such things, you can have lots of fun at your parties just sitting around talking and listening to records, playing interesting games, cooking fudge, spaghetti or other good things, or learning the latest dance steps. Know the limitations of your age group and stay within your boundary line.

IS SMOKING A HABIT?

Smoking is a habit that many teenagers have accepted, disregarding danger reports. If you stayed away from this habit, for life, it still wouldn't be long enough. However if all the others smoke and you feel you just must take up this habit to belong, discuss smoking with your parents. If your approach is right, you may get permission. If you've reached the age and permission is given, for heaven's sake smoke like a lady. This is one habit that most men have long despised in women. Their complaint is that "women smoke like men."

There is an art to smoking. Like everything else you do, you must be attractive at all times.

If you smoke, have your own supply. Passing and sharing a cigarette not only looks bad, but is unsanitary and unhealthy. If you're in the company of a boy and he offers you a cigarette, it doesn't mean that he expects you to smoke. If you don't, refuse it politely. Your rating isn't going up any higher with him whether you do or do not smoke.

The use of ash trays has too often been abused. Ash trays were made for smokers to use. A girl who smokes must never snuff out a cigarette on the floor. Before you light up make sure an ash tray is nearby. Be careful when you leave a burning cigarette in the ash tray you're using. Place it carefully so it cannot fall off and leave burned marks on furniture.

Protecting your furniture and other household items may come easily, simply because you don't want them mistreated and destroyed. Your friends will do the same, knowing this is the way you feel about the things that are dear to you. Watch closely the actions of the people that visit you. Try not to repeat their bad habits when you return their visit.

BE A PERFECT GUEST

Conversation with adults has never been easy for young people. It is not always easy for adults to talk with youngsters, either. Most times young people clam up and have nothing to say. You must have some talk with the parents of your friends when you visit their home. Never enter without speaking and never leave without saying goodby. If there is a party, adults are somewhere around (or should be). Ask for them, find them and let them know how much you enjoyed yourself. It's true most kids don't like this routine. This is not a "follow the leader" game. It's a matter of what's right and wrong. This is right!

If you're invited to a friend's home for dinner (or just a snack), being late is unforgivable. When people go to the trouble of fixing food, the least you could do is to be on time. Everyone is allowed a little time for emergencies or some last minute details, but fifteen minutes is the limit. If you are a perfect guest, you will probably be invited back (if you arrive on time). Arriving late, to anything, is a very bad habit. There is no such thing as C.P.T. (colored people's time). Someone has to be the first to arrive, and it just might as well be you. And don't be the first to leave. There's a right time for departure. Leave when you think the moment is right, always thank-

ing your friend, her mother and other guests for having
had a good time.

SAYING THANK YOU

It will be a big boost to your personality and charm if you
follow up your visit with a telephone call, again saying
how much you enjoyed yourself. There are several ways
to say thank you. One, by saying it verbally, one by
making a telephone call, as we've suggested, and another
with a "thank you" note. You will find many notes and
cards, with messages already thought out for you, in card
shops. If you look carefully, you will find just the one that
expresses your thought perfectly. But it's much nicer if
you think up your own message and write it in your own
handwriting. These are just some of the many rules of
good manners. When you're not sure about doing what's
right, ask your parents. If they don't know, don't give up
and continue to do the wrong thing. Find the answer
somewhere. Search for books in the library, read your
daily newspapers, ask your school teacher or another
adult. You'll go through life never knowing, if you don't
ask.

EATING IN A RESTAURANT

Eating out in restaurants is a way of life, today. You will
especially want to show off your good manners when you
eat out . . . even at the hot dog stand at the nearby
corner. If you're fortunate enough to eat in a fancy place,
you can't afford to be caught with your good manners not
showing. Take your pick of places to eat. You can go
anywhere. Sit-ins, stand-ins, marches, demonstrations
and other fights have given you the opportunity for en-
trance into any of the finest . . . but never without good
manners. When you find you're the only "one" in the
place, all eyes are on you. You won't be nervous if you

know how to conduct yourself. Don't let us down, it's up to you to help keep the welcome sign out on all doors. Make a good showing and make it possible for others to follow you.

At some very special time, during the year, you will want to go to a very special place with a very special person. Save yourself the embarrassment of being turned away. Insist that your date call for a reservation. With this security, it will be impossible for you to be turned down. The headwaiter will lead you to your table. Let your date do most of the talking. He's paying the bill, he deserves the privilege. After asking for your choice of food, he will place the order. Don't sit there like a mummy, feel free to talk with the waiter, but only if it's absolutely necessary. Order foods that you know you can handle with confidence. It's interesting and exciting to try something new. If you're not sure what the food is, ask the waiter.

Don't pile food high on your fork. Cut your meat only when you need it. Help yourself to moderate mouthfuls. Break your bread and butter it in bite-sized pieces. Follow all the other rules for good table manners. Enjoy yourself and keep your voice down. At the end of the meal, if your face needs repair . . . not at the table. The ladies' room is always in a convenient spot. Don't park there. Remember the very nervous young man you left at the table. Be prepared to leave a tip if an attendant is in charge. These rules are not extra special fancy. They apply whenever and wherever you eat, even if its the neighborhood "soul food" restaurant. Good manners go where you go.

GOOD MANNERS GET GOOD GRADES

The rules of good behavior must be continued in school. Every school has its own set. If you transfer from one school to another, it would be unwise to take rules and regulations from one to another. But in addition to these school rules kindness and courtesy are no different here than they are any place else, and that includes your attitude toward your teachers and principal. Treat others as you would like to be treated, and you'll go far.

School is a place where you spend much of your time. This is the place to get an education and to learn how to act with other people. This is where understanding others begins. This is where you learn the importance of fair play . . . in the classroom . . . in club groups . . . and in sports. This is where your honesty pays off . . . in everything you do and above all with your teachers.

If you become an active part of your school, it will help you to mingle more easily with people outside of your school. Knowing how to be comfortable with people and knowing your manners are what they should be is your first big step to popularity.

TEACHERS ARE HUMAN, TOO

Nobody wants to be branded as an "apple polisher" or "teacher's pet," but you aren't trying to be that when you pay her the respect that she deserves from you. She is there for a good reason and so are you. Take advantage of it. She expects you to be courteous enough to get into your classrooms on time. If for some good reason you were detained, it's up to you to go in quietly and explain your reasons for being tardy. Storming in class out of breath, disturbing the rest of the class, without making explanations to the teacher, will not make you a classroom hero. Nobody likes a classroom pest—even those who encourage them. They may have good reasons for doing so. It can hinder your popularity, you know. As your popularity begins to wane, the other person moves to the top. You are old enough to know right from wrong. Let your conscience be your guide!

Your teacher is a human being just like you. If you think she's crabby, irritable, hard to get along with, your actions in the classroom might be the reasons for her disposition. Remember she's there to teach you and you're there to learn. Teachers say it's very upsetting when the entire class must suffer from the actions of one person. Why hinder the progress of others? Your progress in the future depends on the progress you make in school.

If it takes you longer to catch on than it does others, talk it over with your teacher. She will give you extra help, or see that you get it. The more you cooperate with her, the better job she will do, the more you'll learn and the better job you'll do later on when you're out of school.

When questions are directed at you, you either know the answer or you don't. It's no disgrace if you don't. Stand up and say so. Handing the teacher a lot of smart talk will only keep the rest of the class back. Your teacher knows what kind of a student you are, you're not fooling her. Talking when you're supposed to be listening is rude. Asking a lot of silly questions trying to "trip the teacher up" isn't smart either.

SITTING PRETTY IN THE CLASSROOM

Smart girls who want to learn and get ahead sit behind their desks like ladies. Sitting sprawled in your seat with your legs extending out into the aisle is a sure way of making little progress in your studies . . . and a good way of not getting asked out for Saturday or Sunday dates. It makes no difference how good you are in your studies; a girl who isn't half as smart as you, but acts as she should, has so many dates she can't handle them all. Take a tip from her. Check your actions, and check your posture behind your school desk. Boys are always looking!

Going from one class to another can be done without a

lot of noise and fuss. When you come face to face with teachers or the principal, if your actions are as they should be, you will not be embarrassed. You don't have to go to pieces when you meet your teachers in the hallway or on the school grounds. A polite greeting is all that is required. If it is their desire to stop and chat with you, do it quietly and intelligently.

Be a part of your school and its activities. Join club groups. Play on the teams, swim with the swimmers, cooperate with the committees. Remember that you, too, have a contribution to make to your school. You may not have as many ideas as the next girl, but don't let this hold you back. You may work better than she does. Getting along in a group is important, and your ability to listen to another's suggestion and follow through on it shows good sportsmanship. Don't pull out of things just because you don't always get your way. If you have confidence in your plan or suggestion, be big enough to speak up and tell the reasons why.

Being a part of your school and working for its program will strengthen the contribution you will make to your community.

GOOD MANNERS PAVE THE WAY

Your manners on the street are probably the ones that attract the greatest attention. Loud laughing and cutting up on the street attracts attention, and it is uncultivated and vulgar. Wild running and jumping is unnecessary while going back and forth to school. When on the street, or using public transportation, and traveling with a group, pair off in twos and threes and act as well-mannered young ladies should.

When a boy accompanies you down the street, you will want more than at any other time to be letter-perfect in everything you do and say. You can only demand respect from a boy when you, yourself, know what is right and wrong. Give him time and allow him the privilege of being a gentleman. Boys complain that girls are always too quick to do things for themselves . . . like opening the car door, when you get in or out. They say that before they have a chance, girls jump off the bus first, or go through the door first . . . leaving them behind lost and helpless. Girls don't give them a chance to be courteous.

BOYS LIKE WELL-MANNERED GIRLS

If you like the boy you're with, he knows it without you waiting till you get him in public to tell him so. Holding hands, petting and necking on the street and in public conveyances just isn't done. These actions never have and never will be considered good manners. Actually you know better, but many girls want to take advantage of every opportunity to express to a boy how they feel about him. There are many other ways. I'm sure he'd appreciate not being made a spectacle of in public. If the encouragement comes from him, then it's up to you to let him know, without embarrassment and hurt feelings, that this is not the place for such carrying on.

Eating on the street is a bad habit that is too common and one that should be stopped. Walking down the street with a mouthful spoils your entire appearance. Eating hearty hero sandwiches, hamburgers or hot dogs is fine at a baseball or basketball game, but when they are eaten on the street it indicates that you've been neglectful in the good manners department. If you must eat peanuts on the bus or train and they are unshelled, don't drop the shells in a pile at your feet. Put them back into the bag. Would you want to clean up such a mess that someone else had left? No? Well, put yourself in the cleaning person's place. He doesn't want to either.

Cracking popcorn and popping chewing gum in the ear of the person next to you on a crowded subway, bus or in a movie is an invitation to insults. Save your popcorn for later. You don't have to let everybody on the bus know that you're chewing gum. Smacking and popping on it is ugly and distasteful. Also if it is done with too much vigor, it can do horrible things to the shape of your mouth and the beauty of your face. When you are through with your gum, discard it. Don't park it and hope to come back for it, or drop it on the street.

"SUNDAY GO TO MEETING" MANNERS

Whether you attend church regularly or just on special occasions is entirely up to you. Whenever you do go, leave any bad habits that haven't been broken behind you. Church is not a place for horsing around. You go there for one specific purpose (or you should)—spiritual guidance. If you have any other ideas, stay at home.

If you've never been on time anywhere in your life, please arrive punctually for whatever it is you're attending within the church. If for some good reason you didn't quite make it, enter as quietly as possible. Talking, eating and greeting your friends is unforgivable. If you see a friend, a nod of your head or a smile is all you need do to let her know it. Save your conversation for after church service, and even that should be done with consideration. If you have to nibble and chew to keep awake through the service, you never should have come in the first place.

Dressing for Sunday service must be done with moderation. Party clothes are for parties. Cocktail dresses are for cocktail parties or dress-up functions. Wide picture hats are for garden parties or weddings. Brimmed hats the size of wagon wheels that obstruct the view of those unlucky enough to sit behind you were not designed for you to wear to church. Taking space from someone else by placing your personal belongings in the next seat is selfish.

Respect the church and be considerate of those around you and behind you. Decide on costumes and accessories that are neat and attractive . . . in good taste on you.

FULL TIME MANNERS

If you have a full time job or one where you go after school or on Saturdays, take your good manners along with you. Combine your good sense with them and you'll make a fine showing. It is true, business manners differ in many ways from social manners. So if you're working for the first time, keep your eyes and ears open. You will learn how things are done. What you do here may not be done anywhere else. Etiquette in one office may differ entirely from another. Watch the things that go on around you. Listen to what is said and how it's said. If you're old enough to work, leave your childish, school girl manners at home or on the school ground.

Your consideration of others is just as important in business as in other places. Remember you will be treated as you treat those people working with you.

13

The Way You Talk

The girl most likely to succeed in anything she chooses is the girl with a voice that is as feminine and charming as the girl herself (or the girl she is trying to be).

Naturally you want to make a good impression. A big help in that direction is the cultivation of a voice without harsh rasping tones. Everybody admires a girl who looks well and speaks well.

It would take you a long, long time and hard practice really and truly to change the texture of your voice, but checking the tone of it and the correction of your speech can become a daily habit. Have you ever heard the sound of your voice? What did you think about it? Were you satisfied with what you heard? If you're like most people who have had this experience, you didn't like yourself at all.

LISTEN TO YOUR VOICE

The tape-recording machines today make it possible to hear your voice without even leaving your own living room. If you're this fortunate, your self-training speech program will be easy. This is a wonderful way to get accustomed and acquainted with the way you sound, and speech improvements will soon be noticeable. You become aware of where to place heavy accents and when and where to raise and drop the pitch of your voice.

The way your voice sounds to you is not the way it sounds to others. It's not only what you say but the way it sounds to your listeners that really counts. Take a simple phrase like "Where were you?" See how many different ways you can say it with a different intonation each time. You can say it with anger . . . with worry . . . with fear . . . and with annoyance. Your voice will match your mood, and the tone of your voice can give a meaning other than the one you intend to give. Keep your voice under control. Whatever you say—when you say it—your words must ring clear with a crisp distinct sound. Keep your pitch reasonably low, but speak so you are understood.

Some men and women faced with the task of public speaking use the recording system. This helps them cultivate a flawless rhythm that is as pleasing to the ear as a popular musical tune. They listen carefully to their voices and to the pronunciation of each word. They know when to emphasize and where to place accents. These speeches are repeated time and time again until they are perfect in every detail. Speaking is an art. So is conversation, for that matter. Everybody can't be a public speaker or a brilliant conversationalist, but with careful study of your voice and how it sounds, your words and how you speak them, you will be able to talk to anybody at any time.

WORDS WITH A CLEAR RING

Although the recording system is good and can be of tremendous help, it is not an absolute necessity. It's fun to hear your own voice, but you can cultivate a pleasant voice even if you don't hear it recorded. Listening to the things you hear around you is a great help in correcting and improving your speech. Use the time you listen to your radio and watch television . . . study the pronunciation of each word you hear. Not only is this a good way to assist you in improving the sound of your voice and clarifying your speech, but it can be a wonderful vocabulary builder.

LAZY LIPS

Speech is important! Oliver Wendell Holmes said, "Talking is one of the fine arts . . . the noblest . . . the most important!" Analyze your voice and your speech. Work hard on the words that give you trouble. Repeat words you have trouble pronouncing. Work hard on each one until it rings clear. Constant practice will help you overcome a thick heavy sound. Break yourself of the habit of clipping and chopping your words, or letting letters run into each other. Give your words the full form and the roundness they each deserve. Yeah instead of a clear-cut yes, willya instead of will you, and haveya instead of have you, are bad speech habits.

Don't be unfair to the "g" that rightfully belongs to words like going, running, playing and sitting. They too often sound like goin, runnin, playin, and sittin. The "g" adds a special beauty to these words when they are pronounced fully and distinctly. You may have something very interesting to say, but if you can't say it intelligibly, the meaning is lost. All the knowledge bottled up inside you means nothing if you can't share it with others. You may be a very smart girl at your books, but the moment somebody says something to you, you go to pieces and you're lost for words. If you're such a person you need help, and you can help yourself.

READING HELPS

You may be a girl who does a lot of reading. This could be one of the reasons why so much is bottled up inside. You've never given yourself the opportunity to open up and talk. Maybe you've stayed too long by yourself . . . reading and doing things alone. You can help yourself by reading aloud. Good practice comes from reading to the small fry in the family. As you do so, listen carefully and closely to your voice and the sound of your words. The sound of your voice, heard often, will remove those fears that surround you, when it's your turn to talk.

OPEN UP AND SPEAK

Conversing with others is the best way I know to build new friendships. Listening is fine, but you have to say something once in a while, too. Being afraid to talk puts limits on your personality. Talking over and around the listener makes it difficult for that person to hear and understand what you're saying. It's just as bad, if not worse, to talk to or over your shoulder. Why bother? It can't answer you back! Learn to look the person in the eye when you speak; it's a sure indication of security and confidence, when you do.

A real charmer is one who always speaks in a moderately low sweet voice. A whiner and a dripper can be irritating and a real bore. It's annoying to have a girl around who whines when she talks. A phony voice that drips with sugar is also a nuisance. Girls with such voices are usually caught jabbering away with a lot of silly talk. Boys become discouraged very quickly when girls don't really say something . . . something important or interesting. It's important to you and your future, each time you open your mouth to speak, that you make sure what you say makes sense and is worthwhile.

Jokes are all right in their place, but you can tire very easily of the girl who is always making them. On the other hand, don't be a sour puss. There's a limit to your seriousness. Be quick to see the funny side of things. Be good-humored. There will be less danger of hurt feelings.

Practice some worthwhile conversations at home. Converse with your parents and the rest of the household. Friendly conversation with neighbors is good pronunciation practice. Daily use of simple distinctive phrases, in familiar surroundings, will help you express your thoughts when the surroundings are unfamiliar.

KEEP SLANG IN ITS PLACE

Slang words can become a habit. When you talk with school chums, you may get by with sentences full of slang words, but if you're not careful, they become a part of your daily speech. If you must use slang words, be clever enough to know when and where to use them. Your speech, like your dress, must be correct for every occasion.

Feed your mind with interesting information and you'll always have something to add to a conversation. Reading your local newspaper is one of many ways to keep yourself well-informed about current and world events. If you miss the sports page you may find yourself at a loss for words when you want badly to keep the conversation rolling with boys.

NOBODY LIKES A GOSSIPER

Keep your conversations free of gossip. No one likes a gossip, and especially boys. The girls may act as if they do, but as they listen your rating in their estimation begins to drop. If you talk about one girl, you'll talk about another, they think. Before you know it, if you carry gossip you'll be dropped from the crowd. If you can't say something nice, don't talk at all.

Vulgarity must never find its way into your conversation. You can be mad enough to "kill" and still you can express that anger without the use of vulgar words. Don't think you can escape the brand of flip, fresh and unladylike if you use such words even once. What if the boys do use them? Must you do the things boys do? They like you for being girls! Don't copy them. It's the boys you're trying to please . . . remember!

THE TELEPHONE EXPECTS COURTESY

One place where teen-agers talk perhaps more than any other is on the telephone. The telephone is a vitally important instrument, not a toy. It is no longer considered a luxury, but a necessity in modern living. You must learn to treat it that way. In some areas, you pay for every minute you talk over the allotted three- or four-minute period. If you had to pay the telephone bill, you'd be more considerate. Did you ever think your parents might want to use it once in a while? Give them a chance. When speaking on the telephone, cut your conversations short. Say just the things that are necessary, don't abuse your privilege of visiting on the family telephone.

Some young people are frightened stiff when they have to use the telephone. This is particularly true for many on their first job where answering the telephone is one of their duties. If you have worked before and you've had experience in answering business telephones, it is still best to ask the person in charge how the telephone is to be answered, with each new position.

Your voice registers very clearly over the telephone. Every flaw, every sound is heard on the other end of the wire. It is your job to see to it that the message gets through to the other person clearly, distinctly, with the proper fullness given to each sound of each word. You don't have to talk loud and fast over the telephone. Your words should travel at a rate of speed that can be clearly understood. Talking too slowly can be a real drag and talking too fast has a tendency to come through all jumbled up with no meaning.

When you're expected to take telephone messages, never trust your memory. Write everything down, even at home. It is a good idea to repeat it to the person from whom it is taken; then you know you have it right. Write it out clearly and hand it to or leave it for the person it is meant for. If you're the front man for someone else, get as much information as possible from the person calling, before you put the call through.

When answering your phone, make sure your voice is one with a smile. You never know who's on the other end. It may be the call you've been waiting for. Courtesy is always important. Put yourself in the other person's shoes. He has no way of knowing what goes on at your end of the wire. Treat him with telephone good manners, just as you'd like to be treated.

14

The Way You Stand, Walk, and Sit

The big question staring you in the face is what to do with this new improved you. SHOW IT OFF! Of course you're proud of all the work you did. Why hide it? Walk around with pride. Let the world see a new you. The movements of your body will express your happiness, not to mention what your new personality will do. Don't worry too much if you're still not too satisfied with your facial beauty. No one is . . . really! Do not let this get you down. Straighten up and show off all the other beautiful things about you.

Good posture is an important part of your looks and correcting it must be included in your good grooming routine. If your posture is poor and your body is out of line, your body muscles become flabby and begin to sag. This can happen even during your young years, and stay that way for the rest of your life. Poor posture and lazy body movements add an unattractive look to your appearance and your clothes are not shown off to best advantage. But if you stand straight and tall, you look good and feel that way all over. If you train the movements of your body to do the most for your clothes and your figure, the firmness you build now can carry you through life. With all these things in your favor, why shouldn't you feel good? You're proud of yourself, because you know the picture of you is one of poised loveliness.

GOOD POSTURE

If you think you're too tall or too short or too fat or too skinny, good posture can help you look better . . . all over. Don't let any of these things stand in the way of a lovelier you. If you're a little too heavy, you may not move as quickly as you'd like, but still there's no reason for poor posture. If you throw your weight around in barrel-like fashion, rolling and wobbling along, this will tire you out more quickly than walking correctly. Bad posture can play havoc with your figure. But good posture can make an imperfect figure look better. An already good figure will look its best.

If you're short, think and walk tall. Strange, but you'll look inches taller. If you're already tall (and there's no such thing as being too tall), don't let bad posture habits spoil your good fortune. Everyone wants to be tall, so why should you complain?

Test yourself for good posture. Back up against a wall. Straighten out your body with head, shoulders, buttocks, and calves of legs and heels touching. Your chest is out and your chin is up. Relax your shoulders. If you're tight and stiff, you will tire out quickly. Now, move away from the wall keeping this posture. Don't droop! Stay straight and tall; take a look at yourself in a long mirror. See how different you look. It feels strange, doesn't it? Walk around the room. You will feel awkward and stiff, at first.

Continue this test every day and in a short time you can lift your body right up in good position, and you can move your body with easy grace and comfort. If you're one of those girls that pouches out in the back, your next step is to TUCK IN! This is really hard. But you must try until you've mastered it and the back of you is straight and your buttocks are smooth and shapely.

WALK LIKE A MODEL

If you're satisfied with your posture and the way you look standing still, walking should be easy. Keep your body in that straight, upright position. With practice you'll soon be walking like a prima ballerina. Beauty and poise are judged by how little you move your body . . . not how much. The way you walk expresses the way you feel. On those sick days, you can't hide it, for it shows in your walk. But when you feel good, you walk with a snap.

Your body must be flexible as you walk. If your muscles are stiff and taut, your movements are awkward. It is vulgar to wiggle and shake. Don't let anybody fool you, if it's attention you're seeking, you'll get plenty of it, but followed by unkind and undesirable remarks.

You always have an audience. There are thousands of eyes on you each day. It is to your advantage to carry yourself gracefully with easy movements. The flexibility of your muscles is important but your body must be controlled. The way you move your feet helps you with this control. Models are taught from the beginning to stand in what is called the model's foot position. Their feet are always in this position, making their walk graceful and easy. This has been adopted by other women and girls who want the same graceful movement.

Why don't you try it? Put the weight of your body on one leg. Point that foot at a slight angle. The heel of the other foot is placed at its instep with toes pointed in the other direction. The weight of the body remains on the leg in the back. Take it from me, this will not be easy in the beginning. Stay with it! Lift the front foot gently and gracefully and walk. Place the front of the foot to the floor first. The other leg comes, gracefully, around placing itself slightly in front of the other. Always keep the feet placed at a slight angle. If your toes are pointed straight ahead, you will wobble from side to side when you walk. With toes pointed, slightly to the right or to the left, you glide along, moving proudly.

PICKUP AND TURN

It's easy when you want to turn. Just lift your foot, the one in front, and turn. If you've done this correctly you'll find a surprise waiting for you. Look down! Your feet are back in the basic foot position. When you're ready to walk, your steps should not be too short, and neither should they be long lanky strides. The distance of your step should measure about the length of your foot. It's impossible to keep your body in line if your steps are too long and deep. And steps that are too short and too quick are unnatural. Even if hemlines are narrow, walking can be done gracefully and naturally. Pick up your feet . . . don't shuffle. Your legs move from your hips into a graceful swinging motion. Keep those hips still. If they wobble from side to side, your posture is poor and your walk is unattractive. You need more practice. Keep at it, until your walk looks and feels perfect.

If you have been walking all your life with your toes pointed in (pigeon-toed) or with them pointed out (slew-footed), this too can be corrected, if you start now. Don't allow the bones to set too comfortably in this position. If the condition is serious, you may need more correction than I can help you with. But try walking with your toes going in the opposite direction to that which they take now. If they go out, walk with them in. If they go in, walk with them out. Practice this walking around the house. You can't do it on the street at first, you will look too ridiculous.

CARRY YOUR ARMS GRACEFULLY

Your arms can help you move gracefully. They should be relaxed and kept fairly close to your body, moving gently with the motion of your feet. No swinging! If your arms dangle and fall to the front of you, you're curving in the wrong place. Your shoulders are humped and bent, throwing the arm socket out of line with the rest of your body. If they hang in, close to your side, this will let you know that your shoulders are up and back where they should be.

HOW DO OTHERS SEE YOU?

Have you ever watched a crowd of people rushing and scurrying about? Did you check the bad posture and ungraceful body movements? How many times have you seen women who stand gracefully but move grotesquely? The first thought that enters into your mind is, I wonder how I look to other people? Practice different standing positions at home. Walk around the house just as though you were walking before the judges of a beauty contest. If you need advice and suggestions, discuss your carriage problems with your best girl friend or a member of your family.

It will be fun working together—and even more so if it's with your mother. Make her feel proud of the way you've learned to walk. She's been telling you all these years to "pick up your feet." You've had it! Now you're doing better. It's such a happy feeling to know that your mother is always around, with her eyes on you. It's not always easy to take criticism from others, and this is worse when it's your mother. If we could only see ourselves as others see us, what an improved group we'd be.

POSTURE IS IMPORTANT

Keeping your good posture may be more difficult than walking, and especially if you've been accustomed to falling and flopping when you sprawl (not sit) into a chair. Not only is this bad for your body—just think what a beating the chair is getting. If your body is kept in the straight line we've talked about, sitting in a chair is as simple as bending your knees and putting your body down easily into the chair. The muscles stay right where they belong, getting tighter and firmer with every bend. Winding and twisting your body in weird shapes just make it harder to straighten up, once you're on your feet again. You only think you're comfortable. Even in the chair, you can't stay in any one of these positions very long. You can't breathe properly. Your feet and legs become numb from dangling over the arm of the chair. The blood isn't free to circulate properly. You get back aches and sore muscles, your shoulders become round, and generally your body gets into a deep slump and that's the way it stays. It just doesn't make good sense to spend time correcting your standing and walking habits if you're going to allow this lovely you to fall apart when you sit.

It's so easy to put your body close to the seat of the chair, letting your leg muscles support your weight as you lower yourself. If your back does not touch the back of your chair comfortably, adjust yourself until it does . . . slip back with one graceful motion. Curling up with a good book once in a while is great as long as these curling up traits don't turn into bad sitting habits. If this happens too often when you're without your book, you won't know what to do with your hands and legs. They can really get in your way, especially when you're out in company.

When you feel uncomfortable, you begin to fidget. Pulling and fussing will not add to your charm and grace, but to your discomfort. It will help you to overcome these nervous habits if you have something in your hands to give you support. A small handbag resting in your lap is always good. Maybe it's just a handkerchief to put you at ease. Whatever it is, hold it gracefully and whatever you do, don't twist or wind it.

Position is everything in life. Make sure the one you take is a good one. Knees must never be apart when you sit. When you're wearing slacks, you look better if your knees are together or crossed at the ankle. Skirt lengths, long or short, will help in the decision about crossing your legs. With skirts higher than thighs, you look better with both feet on the floor. If your skirt length is one that will allow you to cross your legs without too much exposure, you won't be embarrassed if undergarments give you enough protection.

Taking the right position . . . walking . . . standing . . . or sitting, you will always look like a picture of complete composure and comfort.

15

How Do You Spend Your Spare Time?

"An idle mind is the devil's workshop" . . . a phrase handed down through the years, is one that may be completely new to your ears. Think about it! There's more to it than meets the eye. Behind each one of those words is a lot of truth.

When you're sitting around, with nothing to do, with very little effort, you can get yourself into trouble. If time is put to good use, you generally come through with a good record. It is true, too many girls sit around with time on their hands. Time is valuable! Every moment counts! Believe it or not, your future depends on how you use your spare time, now.

THINK ABOUT YOUR FUTURE

Remember, we said in the very beginning that there is time for everything. Today is the time to lay your foundation for the future. Spare time on your hands can be a big help. Don't just sit around. Plan your future.

Have you given any serious thought to what you want to do when you get older? When you've completed your education? What you want to be? No, it isn't too early to start your plans. It is never too early to think about what you want to do . . . what you want to be. You may change your mind a few times before the decision is final. Giving it some thought, now, will make the decision come sooner.

Remember when you were five? Remember the dreams you had of becoming a nurse, a dancer, a clerk (one that sells all the pretty things you see in stores), a secretary, the only girl who plays in the concert orchestra, a school-teacher, a model, the girl behind the soda fountain, or a mother with four or five children to care for? Maybe by the time you were eight, those dreams had changed and have continued to change a million times right up to the present date. Then, again, maybe they haven't changed at all. If in your mind, you have laid the ground work for your career, put some of your spare time to work for you and your future.

"What do you want to do when you get out of school?" is a question asked of many girls. More than once, the answer is "Get married!" Other girls may think that decision is insane. Anybody can get married! Well, just don't you be so sure. A lot of girls are suffering today because they aren't. Whether it's their fault or the fault of someone else, is their business. Marriage is important and serious. But marriage is not always the answer to a happy, successful future. Don't think marriage is an easy way out. Don't, for one moment, think that getting married is an escape from something that may seem unhappy and unbearable now. Marriage isn't any of these things. Marriage is for people that are ready for it, and not pushed into it. Marriage is for people who understand responsibility and are willing to accept it. Marriage is for people who thoroughly understand themselves and are willing to understand the other person. Marriage is for people who can share . . . share willingly and generously. We could go on and on, but that's enough on marriage. That should give you something to think about. Just remember, if it's marriage you're headed into, without giving it a second thought . . . think about it the second time!

INCREASE YOUR BUDGET

You might be a lot smarter and happier if you tried your hand at earning your own money first. If you plan to go on to college after high school, so much the better. Education can be your life protection. Today, there are many educational opportunities. Take advantage of them. Some of them can be had during your spare time. The more education you have today, the better the job, later on. Business and industry is still looking for qualified young women to fill responsible, high-salaried positions. The color of your skin will not keep you out.

Speaking of education, you may find yourself with or without a college degree. You may or may not be a success with a college education. It will depend on how you put your education to use. Without a college education, you won't necessarily be a failure. Again, it depends on how you use your high school education. Business and industry have no job openings for people without a high school diploma. The most unimportant job will expect that of you.

Have you heard the expression "too many chiefs and not enough Indians"? This only means that everyone wants to be the "boss," the one in "charge," the one to give the "orders." The world is filled with "chiefs." You may never be one. But being a good "Indian" is far more valuable if you do your job well.

But until such time when you're old enough, look at the many ways you can spend your spare time and make it pay off.

Did you know that baby sitting pays off in more ways than one? In addition to watching all your favorite TV programs and listening to records, and catching up on back homework, you get paid for it. There is considerable knowledge to be gained by baby sitting, if you take your job seriously. If you like children, this is a good way to learn more about their habits. If you want to teach, the relationship between you and children will be a good, understanding one. All because of this baby sitting experience. Baby sitting proves an excellent way to learn how to care for your own, later on.

Did you ever consider keeping house for Mother, if for no other reason than making the load a little lighter for her? What a wonderful way this is to train for your future. When you're older, married with a place of your own, it will be easy for you to keep it clean and orderly, because of this experience. Your ability to plan the work and do it, to manage the money (if your parents allow it) and to shop for the groceries and other household needs, will be a great aid to you in the future. If you'd stop complaining about the things your parents ask you to do, and consider their importance to your future, you'd do things a little more willingly. If the family budget will allow it, why not discuss a small allowance for the work you do. This will, at least, give you some extra spending change.

SUMMER TIME IS NOT JUST FOR FUN

When summer comes and you have nothing but time on your hands, you'll be unhappy and bored, if you don't put that time to good use. Don't sit around complaining about "there's nothing to do," making all those around you just as miserable. Summer may be the time for packing up and going away on vacations, but you can get just as much enjoyment making that time pay off for you. Sum-

mer is the time for fun and excitement, it is also the time
for getting things done. Summer can be the right time for
learning. Learning something new. Learn as much as you
can about business. Look into jobs in department stores.
Learn about retailing. Look into banking, insurance. You
might even consider a course on "How to Run a Small
Business." Such a course may bring you big dividends in
the future.

"All work and no fun makes Mary Jane a very dull
girl," you might be thinking. All fun and no work makes
her even duller, I say. Interest yourself in something
constructive, interesting enough to provide achievement
and future success. Naturally, it's all so much more fun
if you work for pay, and you're doing something you like.
Take your hobbies. What do you like to do? If it's knit-
ting, knit items that you can finish quickly and then sell
them. Try your neighborhood church or community center. If you don't know how to knit, learn. It's easy, and
some of the jiffy styles can be finished before two hour-
long TV programs are over. Bake cookies or cakes, make
candy. Sell them to your neighbors. There's nothing
wrong with earning extra money this way.

If you like to shop around in the department stores,
why not try your hand at "personal shopping" for the
neighbors. This might be at the community shopping
center or you may have to travel to the downtown shopping area. Understand just what your "customers" want,
and turn the place upside down till you find it. This is one
of the best ways to train your eyes to top quality merchandise. Help the mothers in your block by walking or
sitting (outside) with the baby, walk the dog, take
clothes to the laundermat. You can take care of two or
three loads at one time. Make some spending money by
running short errands or doing innumerable odd jobs in
your neighborhood. Be your own business manager. Use
your head, and think of what you can do . . . helping
others and helping yourself, at the same time.

If it's mixing sodas or waiting table, try getting a summer or part-time job in the luncheonette or ice-cream nook nearest you.

Run errands for the corner druggist, if you like being around bottles filled with interesting liquids and colored pills. Helping with the stock and keeping merchandise records will take a big load off the shoulders of the owner of that dress shop in your neighborhood. What a break you'll get by being so close to all those pretty clothes. Perhaps if you do a good job, they may let you buy some at a reduction. At the end of summer, the proprietor may not be able to get along without you . . . and an after-school job is in the offing. Whatever it is you do, do it the best you know how, and continue to learn . . . learn something. It won't hurt, and it will help your future.

SHARE YOUR TIME

Prove that your teen-age group is not all bad as is generally thought. Give some of your spare time to your community. Perhaps you can teach Sunday School, or contribute some of your time to the Community Center, or the playground nearest you. If you like to read, organize a reading group for the little ones. Read aloud to them and allow them some reading practice, by reading back. Volunteer your time for camp counseling. Enjoy camp life and learn how to work with younger children. Join club groups at the "Y," in the Girl Scouts, and at the Community Center. Share your interest by being with other girls your age . . . benefit by theirs.

Maybe it's been a real struggle for your parents to keep you in school. Why not show your appreciation in some way? If you're not working to supplement the family budget, you might use your spare time to brush up on subjects that you're weak in. Improve your grades by doing some extra school work. If you're interested, there are many classes you can enroll in. Check your local newspapers and schools.

Why just hang around with nothing to do? Take some

of your time to become familiar with your local library. It's interesting to know how books get to the shelves, and where to look for those you want. Don't be afraid to ask questions of the librarian. Study the library's displays. Attend the discussion groups that gather there. Listen to the lectures. Ask questions and learn! If you like books and do a more than average job of reading, find out about jobs in the library.

Learn a foreign language. Study with records or enroll in a free language class . . . there are some . . . just look around you! Interest some of your friends in a language club. It's more fun, if you all learn to speak another language at the same time.

TAKE ADVANTAGE OF WHAT'S FREE

So many good things in life are free. They are not for just a few, but for everybody. Take advantage of the public park programs, study art exhibits, learn more about the zoo, visit the museums, learn more about what goes on in your community and your city. All this will not cost you one cent.

If you're interested in business and you want to know what makes it tick, the business machines companies will be delighted to have you visit their showrooms. Study the new machines, and there are many, and operate those you're interested in.

Watch your newspapers for listings of fashion shows and fashion and grooming lectures, if you're interested in sewing. Get yourself in one of the free costume designing classes. Listen to the beauty experts as they tell of new beauty products in the department stores or in your neighborhood beauty salon.

If you live in or around New York City, visit the United Nations, and do it often. Sit in on some of the sessions. It will take many trips to know what really goes on behind those large, thick glass walls. Learning never stops.

Improve your body as well as your mind. Join the swimming group . . . play on the basketball team . . . try your swing on the tennis court . . . or be great in another sport. Take some of your time to keep fit.

MAKE A PRETTY ROOM

With your parent's permission, you might like to try your hand at home decorating. Instead of complaining about the place where you live, make it attractive. A house is not always the home you'd like it to be. Home is where you live, so make it a bright happy place to be.

It's easy to paint walls. Give them new life by putting on a coat of a new favorite soothing color. Put some color in your life and change a drab, dull looking room to one that is newly alive with brightness. Select a color that is relaxing and happy to live with.

If you've been given a free hand, change your room from a real bedroom to one that's for sleeping only at night. During the day it's made up into a bedroom-sitting room. Make it a room where you can entertain and be with your friends. This is an ideal arrangement if the rooms are limited and the family group is large. This may be the only space, in the house, where you really feel "at home" . . . in your own little world . . . with privacy and total comfort.

Here is another reason for earning your own money. You can have just the things you want in this world of yours . . . your own radio, television set, record player, hair dryer, your own books and all the gadgets and things that make you relaxed and happy.

Add excitement to the windows by making new curtains and drapes from bright fabric or decorative paper that comes by-the-yard just like cloth. If a line is drawn by your parents and you must keep your creative ability within the confines of your own room, there's much you can do there. Do a little each day, and in no time your own little castle has taken on a completely new look . . . adding new excitement, new enthusiasm and a new look for you.

Rearranging the furniture can make things look different. And nothing gives a room a lift quicker than the addition of bright pictures and flowers. The flowers need not be fresh and the supply doesn't have to come every other day or so. Save your pennies and buy a plant. It can be fake or real. Artificial flowers are better than nothing. Select those that have a fresh-cut look. Skip those that are dead give-aways. Keep them clean and dust free, they'll be bright and "real" looking for a long time.

Once things are to your liking, you will not be ashamed to have your friends in your home, even if it's just your best girl friend. Whatever are your new plans, keep your home clean. Be proud of it!

These few suggestions, we both know, don't even start to scratch the surface of the hundreds of things you can do with the time on your hands. Whether you have a lot or very little, make sure you use it wisely.

16

Your Future

Stop, for a moment, and give some thought to your future and how it looks, from here. Take it from me, your future was never brighter. Doors of opportunity have been opened for you. Others have, at least, been cracked . . . waiting for you to come on in. Others before you have paved the way down many a successful avenue, wanting you to follow in their footsteps.

BRIGHTER THAN EVER

You might not want to hear, again, what you've heard over and over again. But here goes anyway. The doors and roads of opportunity and success will never be touched by you unless you're prepared to face the challenge. Once the opportunity has been given you, you must produce. You can be a part of any working area you desire. You have the right to the job, if you've been properly trained for it. Be positive about accepting the responsibility.

One thing you do know, now, is that you are no longer a child. As you grow older, your mind, your body and your actions begin to make real changes. Things you did a few years ago, you wouldn't be caught doing today. You can't go too far wrong if you remember to always act your age and know your limitations. Look at the unattractive actions of older women that are down right silly, and make sure you are never guilty of the same. Think of the times you've frowned on their teen-age actions, when they should have been acting like adults. Remember how they looked in clothes that belong to your age group? Remember those baby-doll hairdos, better suited for a ten year old, remember how they were not able to handle their drinks and the unbecoming way they handled their cigarettes, and the loud boisterous voices they spoke in on the street? Remember how you've always promised yourself, you'd never be like this. May I remind you, please, always keep this promise. Growing older gracefully can be done in easy simple stages. It's nicer if you can grow younger looking as you grow older. That's a neat trick, if you can do it. But if you're clever, you will allow yourself to grow lovelier, from head to toe, as you grow older.

BOYS MAKE IT EXCITING

Since men play such an important role in the lives of women, how can we part without asking you, "What about the boys in your life?" You're not too young to think about boys. You might be too young to think about them seriously . . . and that's good! But when your mind starts to run seriously on the subject, you must know what you're doing before you can select the boy who will play an important part in your life and your future. There's a man for every woman, so they say. But the woman must know what she wants and what to look for in the guy in her life. Too many girls are influenced only by good looks, or achievement in sports, education, family background or simply by the way a boy dances, or the line he hands her (but what she doesn't know is that he hands the same line to every other girl he sees). Some of these things impress you because you want to be seen with a boy you can be proud of. But not one of those reasons, alone, should be the reason for you to "flip your cool" over any one boy. Who wants to keep a date with a big hunk of he man who can't dance . . . has no personality . . . can't hold a minute and half conversation . . . or one who is a real drag with the other kids? Who needs this kind of man around? Who cares about his good looks? A boy not half so good looking but who knows what to say and do is the one you'll enjoy more.

GOING STEADY

The boy you select should be one who will respect you, at all times. Hunt for one who knows how to protect you, in any situation. A fellow you feel secure with is the one for you. This guy doesn't have to be a steady. I think girls are getting wiser, today. Going steady is not as important as it used to be. There's another group, however, that feel out of things unless they have the same boy, date after date, to hang on to. Is going steady so very important? What does it really mean?

The phrase "going steady" means something different in every set. But let's face it, steady means stable, constant, regular. In your group it may mean "for a short time" until somebody you like better comes along and in another group it may mean "forever." It can mean that you have fallen in love. This is the man of your dreams and there will never be another (so you think). The two of you are perfectly mated. You want to spend all of your time together. It can mean security dates. You no longer have to worry about being left out of the week-end fun, or not being a part of the school prom, because, at last, you've got somebody you can depend on. Here's a boy who will always be around when you need him. He's your steady! It can mean, nothing more, than, "Well, everybody else goes steady, so why shouldn't I?"

Anyway you look at it, and whatever it means in your set, it's serious and it's important. Important enough for you to think seriously about it before you decide to be tied down to one man. That sounds final, doesn't it? Well, if going steady keeps up, it may be. Some steady romances end up in marriage, even though that wasn't the plan in the beginning, and many such marriages are not successful.

Getting pinned or wearing a boy's ring is the end for some girls. Even this doesn't give you the tight hold you'd like to have when you're sporting a boy's frat pin or wearing his school ring. If a boy is really serious he wouldn't give it up unless he knew you were the girl for him. But some boys think, "there's more where that one came from," and give a girl a ring or a pin just to get her off his back. Don't be a girl that pressures a boy out of his proud possession when he doesn't truly want you to have it. You look good in your crowd while you're wearing it, but just think how you'll look to them, when you have to face up to the real reason why it's being worn by another girl.

MAKE YOUR OWN DECISIONS

Don't allow yourself to get pulled in to things that you know very well will lead to trouble. Going steady for a long period of time can do just that, unless you're careful. A boy that you're seeing all the time, can't control his emotions forever, you know. Before you realize what's happening, you begin to give in . . . how can you refuse the demands he makes on you? You're that way about each other, remember? When it's too late, you just might find yourself tied down to a man for the rest of your life . . . and the wrong man! After a relationship with a boy you feel very close to or one you hoped to marry someday, and that day never came, your life could be very lonely raising a child you didn't plan for and never wanted in the first place.

Some girls feel they have to give in to be "in." They couldn't get a steady otherwise. Other girls say they have sex with boys they don't seriously like, but do so because the boy was kind, affectionate, and made them feel like there never was and there never will be another like him. Some boys are sneaky, that way. They have a way of making you feel wanted and loved. Being this close and steady with a boy spells TROUBLE in bright lights. Some girls get roped in and others go in with their eyes wide open. If you don't want your future ruined, keep your eyes wide open and don't get into trouble you can't get out of easily.

BE FRIENDS WITH BOYS

Why not give yourself a chance to look the field over and pick the man of your choice? It might be a better arrangement to have boy friends that are pals instead. This gives you a better chance to know when the real thing comes along. Why shouldn't you be in control of your own time? Why should you start now, with a boy hanging around your neck, telling you what to do and when to do it? Spend your time building friendships with several boys. Wouldn't it be a better plan if you had a boy as a companion for the beach? One that is a terrific swimmer and someone you enjoy idling your time away on the sand with? How about a mate for the movies? . . . one that doesn't feel that he has to lure you into a dimly lit theater to neck . . . but goes to enjoy the picture. You might want a partner to take you to parties. One that is a real knockout on the dance floor. Or you might have a special man for outdoor sports. Many a romance got off to a good start at baseball, basketball or football games.

Think about your future seriously before you make a final decision on the man with whom you expect to spend the rest of your life. If you play the field, you may fall in love with any one of the boys you've dated. But you feel more secure when this happens because you know you've had a chance to look around. As your friendships grow, so does romance.

WHAT A KISS MEANS

Once you realize that you like a boy, you will want to let him know how you feel. A kiss will tell him. What's in a kiss, anyway? Trouble if you don't know what you're doing. Sure, you feel this way about him and it's perfectly natural for you to express your affection in this manner. But don't start anything you can't finish. Whether you kiss him or not is a decision that no one can make for you. A kiss can lead to many things. Some boys expect kissing and petting every time they ask you for a date. Don't cheapen yourself by accepting dates like this. If a boy finds that it is easy to neck with you he spreads the news around to the other boys. Boys like to blow off and this kind will blow up the story. When you hear it again, you may be the only one who knows it wasn't like that at all. If you're the fickle type and think necking and petting is fun and makes you popular with the boys, this news spreads, too. Most boys like to feel that the girl he dates is something he considers special. If boys talk about you as being an easy push over before long they all will drop you like a hot potato. Boys talk! More than girls ever dared! Everytime you're out with a boy your reputation is at stake.

BEWARE OF THE WOLF

You're under the wrong impression, if you're silly enough to think that just because a boy petted with you, that you're the only girl for him. These are the guys you have to watch with a keen eye. Be on the watch for the wolf and his whistle. Watch out for the boy who wants to take you to the beach . . . but only at night. The one who knows all the dark secluded spots. The one who never wants to double date or be with the crowd. The one who thinks of nothing else other than petting and necking . . . or whatever it's called in your set. One who is always scheming and planning how to get you in his clutches. He's not so carried away just because you're you. He does this with any other girl he can date. Beware of this wolf and don't get caught in his plan.

Don't be a girl that goes along with all male sugges-tions. Don't worry about your popularity. Who wants to be popular with the wolf? Why risk your reputation. A good one people take for granted. They are like elephants with a bad one . . . they never forget.

MAKE EACH EXPERIENCE COUNT

What you do today, lasts forever! Every experience you have with a boy . . . good or bad . . . you carry with you into your future. You're growing up and life rushes along at a rapid pace. Sometimes things happen so fast, you wonder where they will lead you. Hold on, now! Don't let them carry you too fast. Take full advantage of each experience, each day. Make each one count. Reap the benefits of your young life.

Make sure you know where you're going . . . you only go this way once. Let's face it, your future faces you! Plan for it! Protect it!

Success and good luck!

Index

THE AUTHOR

ELSIE ARCHER is a Texas-born, California-bred New Yorker who is constantly in touch with teen-age girls. She has had wide experience as a career-development assistant and charm-school instructor. As a fashion representative for McCall's Pattern Company, she travels to schools and colleges, participating in good grooming progra ns and presenting fashion shows. Mrs. Archer is also associated with a public relations firm. She has worked in the buying office of I. Magnin & Company and has been fashion editor of *Ebony* magazine.